United Nations Office at Vienna
Centre for Social Development and Humanitarian Affairs

MANUAL ON THE EFFECTIVE PREVENTION AND INVESTIGATION OF EXTRA-LEGAL, ARBITRARY AND SUMMARY EXECUTIONS

United Nations
New York, 1991

Symbols of United Nations documents are composed of capital letters combined with figures. Mention of such a symbol indicates a reference to a United Nations document.

Material in this publication may be freely quoted or reprinted, but acknowledgement is requested, together with a copy of the publication containing the quotation or reprint.

ST/CSDHA/12

UNITED NATIONS PUBLICATION
Sales No.: E.91.IV.1
ISBN 92-1-130142-4
01500P

CONTENTS

Annexes

INTRODUCTION

In many countries throughout the world, extra-legal, arbitrary and summary executions take place undocumented and undetected. These executions include: (a) political assassinations; (b) deaths resulting from torture or ill-treatment in prison or detention; (c) death resulting from enforced "disappearances"; (d) deaths resulting from the excessive use of force by law-enforcement personnel; (e) executions without due process; and (f) acts of genocide. The failure to detect and disclose these executions to the international community is a major obstacle to the rendering of justice for past executions and the prevention of future executions.

This Manual is the result of several years of analysis, research and drafting undertaken because of extra-legal, arbitrary and summary executions throughout the world. Its purpose is to supplement the "Principles on the effective prevention and investigation of extra-legal, arbitrary and summary executions", adopted by the Economic and Social Council in its resolution 1989/65 of 24 May 1989, on the recommendation of the Committee on Crime Prevention and Control, at its tenth session, held in Vienna, from 5 to 16 February 1990.

Concurrent to the elaboration of the Principles, there was concerted action by non-governmental organizations to provide additional guidance in the area of effective prevention and investigation of extra-legal, arbitrary and summary executions, by offering technical advice on the meaningful implementation of the Principles.

The preparation of this Manual was greatly facilitated by the Minnesota Lawyers International Human Rights Committee. At its initiative, an international group of experts in forensic science, lawyers, human rights experts and others volunteered their time and expertise to assist in the preparation of the draft Principles and to provide appropriate follow-up for their implementation, the contents of which constitute the major part of the Manual.

In this connection, special acknowledgement is due to the following:

Medical examiners and forensic pathologists: Dr. Jorgen L. Thomsen, University Institute of Forensic Medicine and Committee of Concerned Forensic Scientists and Physicians for the Documentation of Human Rights Abuses (CCFS), Copenhagen, Dr. Clyde Snow, Forensic Anthropology, Dr. Lindsey Thomas, Dr. Garry Peterson, Dr. Robert Kirschner, Deputy Chief Medical Examiner, Cook County Medical Examiner's Office, Chicago, Dr. Fred Jordan, Chief Medical Examiner, Oklahoma City;

Lawyers: Thomas Johnson, Penny Parker, Robert P. Sands, Gregory Sands, Professor David Weissbrodt, University of Minnesota Law School;

Non-governmental organizations: Barbara Frey, Executive Director, Minnesota Lawyers International Human Rights Committee, Sonia Rosen, Staff Attorney, Minnesota Lawyers International Human Rights Committee, Marie Bibus, Janet Gruschow, Science and Human Rights Program, American Association for the Advancement of Science;

Other specialists: Eric Stover, former Director, Science and Human Rights Program, American Association for the Advancement of Science, Dr. John J. Fitzpatrick, Chair, Division of Trauma Radiology, Cook County Hospital, Chicago, Dr. Karen Ramey Burns, Crime Lab Scientist, Division of Forensic Sciences, Georgia Bureau of Investigation, Decatur.

Appreciation is also expressed to the American Association for the Advancement of Science and the Ford Foundation for their contributions to this publication.

I. INTERNATIONAL HUMAN RIGHTS STANDARDS

A number of international standards outlaw arbitrary deprivation of life. The Universal Declaration of Human Rights, adopted by the General Assembly in its resolution 217 A (III) of 10 December 1948, states that "everyone has the right to life, liberty, and security of person". The International Covenant on Civil and Political Rights, adopted by the General Assembly in its resolution 2200 A (XXI) of 16 December 1966, which was promulgated in 1966 and has been ratified by 87 States, provides in article 6, that "no one shall be arbitrarily deprived of his life". Prohibitions of extra-legal, arbitrary and summary executions are also found in the following instruments: the American Convention on Human Rights, article 4(1): "No one shall be arbitrarily deprived of his life"; the African Charter on Human and Peoples' Rights, article 4: "Every human being shall be entitled to respect for his life and the integrity of his person. No one may be arbitrarily deprived of this right"; and the European Convention for the Protection of Human Rights and Fundamental Freedoms, article 2(1): "No one shall be deprived of his life intentionally save in the execution of a sentence of a court following his conviction of a crime for which this penalty is provided by laws".

The international organs and bodies that have been active in implementing the right to be free from arbitrary deprivation of life include the General Assembly, the Economic and Social Council, the Committee on Crime Prevention and Control, the Commission on Human Rights and its Special Rapporteur on summary or arbitrary executions, the Sub-Commission on Prevention of Discrimination and Protection of Minorities, the Human Rights Committee and the International Labour Organisation; the Inter-American Commission on Human Rights; the African Commission on Human and People's Rights; and the European Commission on Human Rights. Significant action taken by these international bodies to prevent extra-legal, arbitrary and summary executions are discussed below.

A. United Nations

1. General Assembly

The General Assembly of the United Nations, by its resolution 35/172 of 15 December 1980, adopted for the first time a specific resolution on arbitrary or summary executions in which, concerned at the occurrence of the executions that are widely regarded as being politically motivated, Member States concerned were urged to respect as a minimum standard the content of the relevant provisions of the International Covenant on Civil and Political Rights so as to guarantee the most careful legal procedures and the greatest possible safeguards. In resolution 36/22 of 9 November 1981, the General Assembly, bearing in mind the results of the Sixth United Nations Congress on the Prevention of Crime and the Treatment of Offenders (see section A.7, below), condemned the practice of summary executions and arbitrary executions and invited all Member States, specialized agencies, regional, interregional organizations and relevant non-governmental organizations to answer the Secretary-General's request for their views and observations concerning the problem of arbitrary executions and summary executions to be reported to the Committee on Crime Prevention and Control at its seventh session in 1982 (see section A.6, below). In resolutions 37/182 of 17 December 1982, 38/96 of 16 December 1983, 39/110 of 14 December 1984 and 40/143 of 13 December 1985, the Assembly charted a course of action aimed at strengthening the United Nations position against summary or arbitrary executions.

On 4 December 1986, the General Assembly adopted resolution 41/144, strongly condemning the large number of summary or arbitrary executions that continued to take place in various parts of the world. The Assembly also endorsed the conclusion of the Special Rapporteur on Summary or Arbitrary Executions, appointed by the Economic and Social Council in 1982, that it was necessary to develop international standards designed to ensure that investigations were conducted in all cases of suspicious death including provisions for an adequate autopsy (E/CN.4/1986/21).

In its resolution 42/141 of 7 December 1987, the Assembly took an additional step towards encouraging the drafting of international standards by inviting the Special Rapporteur to continue to receive information from appropriate United Nations bodies and other international organizations, to examine the elements to be included in such standards and to report to the Commission on Human Rights on progress made in that respect. The Assembly, therefore, not only recognized that a gap existed in international protection against arbitrary or summary executions, but also stimulated its subsidiary bodies to take an active interest in filling that gap. In doing so, the Assembly has been instrumental in advancing the process of promulgating such new standards. In its resolution 43/151 of 8 December 1988, the Assembly invited Governments, international organizations and non-governmental organizations to support the efforts made in United Nations forums towards the adoption of international standards for the proper investigation of all deaths in suspicious circumstances, including provision for adequate autopsy. Further, the Assembly endorsed the elements proposed by the Special Rapporteur for inclusion in such international standards. Keeping that in mind, the Assembly, by resolution 44/162 of 15 December 1989 endorsed the Principles adopted by the Economic and Social Council and, in resolution 44/159 of the same date, encouraged Governments, international organizations and non-governmental organizations to organize training programmes and support projects with a view to training or educating law enforcement officials in human rights issues connected to their work and appealed to the international community to support endeavours to that end. 1/

In parallel to this work, the Assembly adopted by resolution 39/46, annex, of 10 December 1984, the Convention against Torture and Other Cruel, Inhuman or Degrading Treatment or Punishment, which became effective on 26 June 1987. In its preamble, the Convention referred to the Declaration on the Protection of All Persons from being Subjected to Torture and Other Cruel, Inhuman or Degrading Treatment or Punishment, adopted by the Assembly in resolution 3452 (XXX), annex, of 9 December 1975, on the recommendation of the Fifth United Nations Congress on the Prevention of Crime and the Treatment of Offenders.

That Convention not only specifies that the States Parties will outlaw torture in their national legislation, but also notes explicitly that no order from a superior or exceptional circumstance may be invoked as a justification of torture. The Convention also introduces two new elements of particular significance to efforts by the United Nations to combat torture. The first is that, henceforth a torturer may be prosecuted wherever he is to be found in the territory of any State Party to the Convention, since the Convention specifies that persons alleged to have committed acts of torture may be tried in any State Party or that they may be extradited so that they may be tried in the State Party where they committed their crimes. The second new element is that the Convention contains a provision that allows for an international inquiry if there is reliable information indicating that torture is being systematically practised in the territory of a State Party to the Convention. Such an inquiry may include a visit to the State Party concerned, with its agreement.

The States Parties to the Convention also pledge to take effective legislative, administrative, judicial or other measures to prevent acts of torture in any territory under their jurisdiction. No exceptional circumstances whatsoever, whether a state of war, internal political instability or any other public emergency, may be invoked as a justification of torture.

Under the Convention, no State Party may expel, return or extradite a person to another State where there are substantial grounds for believing that he would be in danger of being subjected to torture.

The States Parties agree to afford one another the greatest measure of assistance in connection with criminal proceedings brought forward in respect of acts of torture, and to ensure that education and information regarding the prohibition against torture are fully included in the training of law enforcement personnel, civil or military, medical personnel, public officials and other persons who may be involved in the custody, interrogation or treatment of any individual subjected to any form of arrest, detention or imprisonment.

The States Parties also undertake to ensure in their legal systems that the victims of acts of torture obtain redress and have an enforceable right to fair and adequate compensation, including the means for as full a rehabilitation as possible. 2/

2. Economic and Social Council

The Economic and Social Council of the United Nations has repeatedly addressed the question of arbitrary or summary executions. For example, the Council has continuously and consistently appealed to Governments, regional intergovernmental organizations and non-governmental organizations to take effective action to combat and eliminate summary or arbitrary executions, including extra-legal executions. The Council has also encouraged and endorsed a number of initiatives to be taken by the human rights and criminal justice bodies of the United Nations, which are described below, aimed at eliminating that alarming and deplorable practice.

3. Commission on Human Rights

Sub-Commission on Prevention of Discrimination and Protection of Minorities of the Commission of Human Rights

In 1987 the Working Group on Detention annexed to its report (E/CN.4/Sub.2/1987/15) to the Sub-Commission on Prevention of Discrimination and Protection of Minorities of the Commission on Human Rights an explanatory paper on the elaboration of norms guaranteeing an impartial investigation into arbitrary execution or suspicious violent death, in particular during detention. Creating norms for autopsy procedures was noted as being particularly useful in determining whether or not a death was suspicious. That report contained also draft standards for the investigation of arbitrary executions, submitted by the International Commission of Jurists.

In its report for 1988 (E/CN.4/1989/3 - E/CN.4/Sub.2/1988/45), the Sub-Commission by decision 1988/109 requested the Secretary-General to provide it with a document describing the work being done in other international forums on international standards for adequate investigations into all cases of suspicious deaths in detention as well as adequate autopsy.

In 1989, the Sub-Commission considered a report of the Secretary-General (E/CN.4/Sub.2/1989/25) summarizing the activities of various United Nations bodies concerning international standards for investigating suspicious deaths, including adequate autopsy.

Two Special Rapporteurs have been appointed at the request of the Commission on Human Rights.

Special Rapporteur on summary or arbitrary executions

In March 1982, the Economic and Social Council by its resolution 1982/35 of 7 May 1982 authorized a Special Rapporteur to study the questions related to summary or arbitrary executions. The Special Rapporteur, Mr. Amos Wako of Kenya, was appointed in 1982 at the request of the Commission on Human Rights, and immediately began the task of collecting information from around the world on summary or arbitrary executions. He has since prepared eight annual reports addressing a wide range of issues concerning summary or arbitrary executions and informing the Commission of his activities, including urgent appeals to Governments.

In 1986, the Special Rapporteur included in his report (E/CN.4/1986/21) to the Commission on Human Rights, consideration of the measures to be taken when a death occurs in custody.

> "One of the ways in which Governments can show that they want this abhorrent phenomenon of arbitrary or summary executions eliminated is by investigating, holding inquests, prosecuting and punishing those found guilty. There is therefore a need to develop international standards designed to ensure that investigations are conducted into all cases of suspicious death and in particular those at the hands of the law enforcement agencies in all situations. Such standards should include adequate autopsy. A death in any type of custody should be regarded as prima facie a summary or arbitrary execution, and appropriate investigation should immediately be made to confirm or rebut the presumption. The results of investigations should be made public (para. 209)."

Referring to the Principles adopted by the Economic and Social Council in its resolution 1989/65 of 24 May 1989, the Special Rapporteur stated that "his position with regard to the implementation of his mandate is strongly supported by this resolution". He will now refer to the Principles in his annual examination of alleged incidents of summary or arbitrary executions. The Special Rapporteur stated further that "any Government's practice that fails to reach the standards set out in the Principles may be regarded as an indication of the Government's responsibility, even if no government officials are found to be directly involved in the acts". He recommended that Governments review national laws and regulations, as well as the practice of judicial and law enforcement authorities, with a view to securing effective implementation of the standards set by Council resolution 1989/65.

This report focused on "the absence of investigation, prosecution and/or punishment in cases of death in suspicious circumstances" (E/CN.4/1986/21). The Special Rapporteur noted that Governments were extremely reluctant to investigate deaths where military or law enforcement agencies were involved. Often, in those cases, as noted by other writers, autopsies or inquest proceedings either did not take place or crucial information, such as evidence of torture, was omitted. 3/

In response to the Special Rapporteur's report of 1987 (E/CN.4/1987/20), the Commission on Human Rights welcomed his recommendation that Governments should review the machinery for investigation of deaths under suspicious circumstances in order to secure an impartial, independent investigation on such deaths, including an adequate autopsy. The Commission also welcomed the Special Rapporteur's recommendation that international organizations should make a concerted effort to draft international standards designed to ensure proper investigation by appropriate authorities into all cases of suspicious death, including provisions for adequate autopsy.

In his 1988 report (E/CN.4/1988/22) to the Commission, the Special Rapporteur devoted an entire section to a discussion on the importance of standards for proper investigation into all cases of suspicious deaths. In particular, he outlined seven elements that should be included as a minimum in such standards: promptness, impartiality, thoroughness, protection, representation of the family of the victim, publication of the findings and an independent commission of inquiry. The Commission endorsed these recommendations.

By its resolution 1989/64 of 8 March 1989, the Commission took note with appreciation of the subsequent report of the Special Rapporteur (E/CN.4/1989/25) and again welcomed his recommendations with a view to eliminating summary or arbitrary executions. Following that with a further report (E/CN.4/1990/22), the Special Rapporteur reviewed new developments in summary or arbitrary executions. He took note of a particularly alarming trend, which was rapidly spreading, of death threats directed, in particular, against persons who played key roles in defending human rights and achieving social and criminal justice. At the same time, however, he noted considerable achievements made by the General Assembly and the Economic and Social Council in areas directly or indirectly related to his mandate.

Special Rapporteur on torture

The Commission on Human Rights decided, in its resolution 1985/33, to appoint a Special Rapporteur to examine questions relevant to torture, requesting him to seek and receive credible and reliable information on such questions and to respond to that information without delay. This decision was subsequently approved by the Council in its decision 1985/144 of 30 May 1985.

The mandate of the Special Rapporteur on questions relevant to torture requests him to report to the Commission, which is composed of government representatives, on the phenomenon of torture in general. To this end, he establishes contact with Governments and asks them for information on the legislative and administrative measures taken to prevent torture and to remedy its consequences whenever it occurs.

The Special Rapporteur is also expected to respond effectively to the credible and reliable information that comes before him. This provision of the Special Rapporteur's mandate has led to the urgent action procedure, which considerably increases the effectiveness of his activities.

The Special Rapporteur's task extends to all States Members of the United Nations and to all States with observer status. He corresponds with Governments, requesting them to inform him of the measures they have taken or plan to take to prevent or combat torture. He also receives requests for urgent action, which he brings to the attention of the Governments concerned in order to ensure protection of the individual's right to physical and mental integrity. In addition, he holds consultations with government representatives who wish to meet with him and, in accordance with his mandate, makes consultation visits to some parts of the world.

For his future activities, the Special Rapporteur recommended to the Commission on Human Rights that:

Detention incommunicado should be declared illegal;

Any person who is arrested should be brought without delay before a competent judge, who should rule immediately on the lawfulness of his arrest and authorize him to see a lawyer;

Any person arrested should undergo a medical examination;

Any detainee who dies should be autopsied in the presence of a representative of his family;

External experts should regularly inspect places of detention.

4. Human Rights Committee

The Human Rights Committee, established under the International Covenant on Civil and Political Rights, article 28, has created a body of jurisprudence in individual cases of arbitrary executions in custody, particularly in connection with the implementation of the relevant provisions of the Optional Protocol to that Convention. In the case of Eduardo Bleier, for example, the Committee considered the allegations by Bleier's mother and wife that he had been held incommunicado and tortured to death by the Uruguayan military. 4/ The Committee refused to accept the Uruguayan Government's denial at face value. Instead, upon receiving evidence from fellow prisoners who had witnessed Bleier's torture, the Committee concluded that he had been tortured in violation of article 7 of the International Covenant on Civil and Political Rights, and that there were serious reasons to believe that the Uruguayan authorities had killed Bleier in violation of article 6 of the International Covenant. The Committee urged the Uruguayan Government to bring to justice any persons responsible for Bleier's death, disappearance and ill-treatment, and to pay compensation to his family for his death.

A further example was that, in April 1985, the Human Rights Committee found the arbitrary executions of 15 opponents to the military ruler of Suriname in December 1982 to constitute an intentional violation of article 6(1) of the Covenant. The Committee urged the Government to take effective steps to investigate the executions, to bring the responsible persons to justice, to pay compensation to the families and to ensure future protection of the right to life. 5/

5. Committee against Torture

The implementation of the Convention against Torture and Other Cruel, Inhuman or Degrading Treatment or Punishment is monitored by the Committee against Torture, which consists of 10 experts of high moral standing and recognized competence in the field of human rights. Under article 19 of the Convention, the States parties submit to the Committee, through the Secretary-General of the United Nations, reports on the measures they have taken under the Convention. Each report is considered by the Committee, which may make general comments and include such information in its annual report to the States parties and to the General Assembly.

Under article 20 of the Convention, if the Committee receives reliable information which appears to it to contain well-founded indications that torture is being systematically practised in the territory of a State Party, the Committee invites that State Party to co-operate in the examination of the information and to this end to submit observations with regard to the information concerned. The Committee may, if it decides that this is warranted, designate one or more of its members to make a confidential inquiry and to report to the Committee urgently. In agreement with that State Party, such an inquiry may include a visit to its territory.

After examining the findings of its member or members submitted to it, the Committee transmits these findings to the State Party concerned together with any comments or suggestions which seem appropriate in view of the situation.

All the proceedings of the Committee under article 20 are confidential and, at all stages of the proceedings, the co-operation of the State Party is sought. After such proceedings have been completed, the Committee may, after consultations with the State Party concerned, decide to include a summary account of the results of the proceedings in its annual report to the other States Parties and to the General Assembly.

6. Committee on Crime Prevention and Control

The General Assembly in its resolution 35/172 of 15 December 1980 requested the Secretary-General to report to the Committee on Crime Prevention and Control at its seventh session, held at Vienna, from 15 to 24 March 1982, on the question of arbitrary or summary executions. By resolution 36/22 of 9 November 1981, the Assembly requested the Committee to examine that question with a view to making recommendations. Having reviewed the report submitted by the Secretary-General (E/AC.57/1982/4 and Corr.1 and Add.1), the Committee recommended to the Economic and Social Council the adoption of a resolution on arbitrary or summary executions.

The Council, in its resolution 1983/24 of 26 May 1983, strongly condemned and deplored the brutal practice of summary executions and decided that the Committee should further study the question of death penalties that do not meet the acknowledged minimum legal guarantees and safeguards, as contained in the International Covenant on Civil and Political Rights and other international instruments.

The Committee at its eighth session, held at Vienna, from 21 to 30 March 1984, elaborated a number of safeguards guaranteeing protection of the rights of those facing the death penalty. The Council adopted the safeguards recommended by the Committee in resolution 1984/50, annex, of 25 May 1984.

The Council, in its resolution 1986/10 of 21 May 1986, section VI, requested that the Secretary-General should submit a report on extra-legal, arbitrary and summary executions to the Committee on Crime Prevention and Control at its tenth session in 1988, held at Vienna, from 22 to 31 August 1988. The Secretary-General submitted a report entitled "Extra-legal, arbitrary and summary executions and measures for their prevention and investigation" (E/AC.57/1988/5). On the basis of discussion at the Committee, including statements made by non-governmental organizations, 6/ the Committee recommended to the Council the adoption of a draft containing the Principles on the Effective Prevention and Investigation of Extra-Legal, Arbitrary and Summary Executions. The Committee has been entrusted with the function of periodically reviewing the implementation of these Principles.

7. United Nations congresses on the prevention of crime and the treatment of offenders

In 1980, the Sixth United Nations Congress on the Prevention of Crime and the Treatment of Offenders in its Caracas Declaration 7/ stressed, inter alia, that "criminal policy and the administration of justice should be based on principles that will guarantee the equality of everyone before the law without any discrimination, as well as the effective right of defence and the existence of judicial organs that are equal to the task of providing speedy and fair justice and of ensuring greater security and protection of the rights and freedoms of all people". In resolution 5 on extra-legal executions, the Congress called upon all Governments to take effective measures to prevent extra-legal executions and urged all organs of the United Nations dealing with questions of crime prevention and human rights to take all possible action to bring such acts to an end.

In 1985, the Seventh United Nations Congress also adopted a resolution on extra-legal, arbitrary and summary executions calling upon all Governments to take urgent and incisive action to investigate such acts, wherever they may occur, to punish those found guilty and to take all other measures necessary to prevent those practices. 8/

B. International Labour Organisation

The Committee on Freedom of Association of the Governing Body of the International Labour Organisation (ILO) reviews complaints alleging the executions of trade unionists around the world. Regarding the deaths of Rudolf Vierra, Mark Pearlman, and Michael Hammer in El Salvador, the ILO Committee requested that the Government of El Salvador transmit the results of the judicial inquiry underway and pursue actively its investigations into these murders. 9/

C. Regional organizations

1. Inter-American Commission on Human Rights

The Inter-American Commission on Human Rights has taken an approach similar to the Human Rights Committee of the United Nations in cases involving arbitrary executions. For example, in Case No. 7481 of 8 March 1982, regarding executions by a military regiment in Bolivia in 1980, the Inter-American Commission found violations of common article 3 of the Geneva Conventions, which had been ratified by the Bolivian Government. The Commission recommended, among other remedies, that the Bolivian Government "order a fuller and impartial investigation to determine responsibility for the excess and abuses ...". 10/

In two landmark decisions, the Inter-American Court of Human Rights found the Government of Honduras in violation of articles 4 (right to life); 5 (right to humane treatment); and 7 (right to personal liberty) of the American Convention on Human Rights. 11/ The Court in the Velasquez Rodriguez Case and the Godinez Cruz Case, 12/ ruled that in cases of "disappearances", "the duty [on the part of the Government of Honduras] to investigate facts of this type continues as long as there is uncertainty about the fate of the person disappeared", and ordered Honduras to pay damages to the families of the victims. Furthermore, the Inter-American Court adopted measures, taken in response to the assassination of two important witnesses, insisting upon the protection of witnesses appearing as part of the investigation.

2. African Commission on Human and People's Rights

The recently established African Commission on Human and People's Rights, a subsidiary body of the Organization of African Unity, has not yet considered any cases involving the arbitrary deprivation of life. The Commission's mandate stems from the African Charter of Human and People's Rights, which provides inter alia that the Commission may enter into written communication with a State Party of the Charter when it is alleged by another State party that the former has violated the provisions of the Charter.

3. European Commission on Human Rights

The European Commission on Human Rights has reviewed fewer cases involving the right to life than the Inter-American Commission. In one case, Cyprus v. Turkey, the European Commission considered whether the Turkish army had engaged in mass executions of civilians at the time of the invasion of Cyprus. The Commission found sufficient eyewitnesses and second-hand testimony from refugees to conclude that there were "strong indications of executions committed on a substantial scale". 13/ The Committee of Ministers took note of the Commission's report and urged talks between the Greek and Turkish communities on Cyprus, but took no further action on the matter.

II. THE ELABORATION OF INTERNATIONAL STANDARDS FOR EFFECTIVE PREVENTION OF EXTRA-LEGAL, ARBITRARY AND SUMMARY EXECUTIONS

The need for an international scientific protocol for the investigation of deaths has been recognized for several years. In 1979, the Danish Medical Group of Amnesty International expressed a desire for established international rules for the completion of death certificates. In 1984, J. L. Thomsen observed that forensic medicine was being practised in different ways, and that common guidelines and definitions would facilitate communications. 14/

Non-governmental organizations emphasized the need for developing and adopting international standards as a practical outcome of their missions to countries where extra-legal, arbitrary and summary executions were alleged to take place. For example, an Amnesty International mission to one country found in 1983 that the procedures of the authorities for recording and investigating violent deaths were totally inadequate for determining the causes of more than 40,000 deaths that had occurred between 1979 and 1984, or for identifying the parties responsible. The procedures were even inadequate to determine the precise number of these deaths.

Similarly, a delegation from the American Association for the Advancement of Science sent to another country to assist in the identification of thousands of persons abducted or killed between 1976 and 1983 concluded that the identification of the remains was beyond the capabilities of local institutions, and recommended the establishment of a national investigative centre with well-trained forensic scientists and a director with independent investigative powers. The delegation, however, was optimistic that even the identification of the remains of a small number of the "disappeared" and a determination of the causes of their deaths could be a significant deterrent if those responsible for the deaths could be identified and brought to justice.

Even when Governments order inquests, investigators often find it difficult to ascertain the facts surrounding arbitrary executions. Eyewitness accounts may be hard to obtain because witnesses fear reprisals or because the only witnesses were those conducting executions themselves. Assassins often conceal their crimes by making their victims "disappear". As a result, bodies of victims are usually found months or years later, buried in shallow, unmarked graves. Disposal in this manner often complicates identification of the body and determination of the cause and manner of death. In some cases, the natural decomposition of the body's soft tissue erases evidence of trauma such as bruising, stab wounds or gunpowder burns. In others, the perpetrators deliberately mutilate the person, either before or after death, in an attempt to thwart identification or to intimidate others.

Most countries have a system for investigating the cause of death in cases with unusual or suspicious circumstances. Such a procedure provides some reassurance that unexplained deaths do not remain unexplained and that the perpetrator is tried by a competent court established by law. In some countries, however, these procedures have broken down or have been abused, particularly where the death may have been caused by the police, the army or other government agents. In these cases, a thorough and independent investigation is rarely done. Evidence that could be used to prosecute the offender is ignored or covered up, and those involved in the executions go unpunished.

To address the need for developing uniform standards, the international community began to formulate a set of principles and medicolegal standards for the investigation and prevention of extra-legal, arbitrary and summary executions. That work, which dates back to the beginning of the 1980s, made

considerable advances with the preparation of the Principles on the Effective
Prevention and Investigation of Extra-Legal, Arbitrary and Summary Executions
recommended by the Committee on Crime Prevention and Control at its tenth
session in Vienna in 1988. The Principles set forth in annex I were adopted
by the Economic and Social Council in its resolution 1989/65, annex, of
24 May 1989 and endorsed by the General Assembly in its resolution 44/162 of
15 December 1989.

It is hoped that observance of the provisions of the Principles will lead
to a decrease of extra-legal, arbitrary and summary executions in two ways.
First, use of the adopted procedures during death investigations should produce
the evidence necessary for increased detection and disclosure of other executions. The persons responsible for such executions can then be held accoun-
table through judicial or political sanctions. Secondly, adoption of the
standards will also provide international observers with guidelines to evaluate
investigations of suspicious deaths. Non-compliance with the standards can be
publicized and pressure brought against non-complying Governments, especially
where extra-legal, arbitrary and summary executions are believed to have occurred. If a Government refuses to establish impartial inquest procedures in such
cases, it might be inferred that the Government is hiding such executions. The
fear of condemnation by the international community may encourage government
compliance with the inquest standards, which, in turn, should reduce extra-
legal, arbitrary and summary executions.

An additional benefit of compliance with these standards is that a Government suspected of involvement in an extra-legal, arbitrary and summary execution would have an opportunity of satisfying the international community, as
well as its own people, that it was not responsible for the death of a particular person or persons. A Government's compliance with these standards,
regardless of the outcome of an inquiry, may increase confidence in the rule
of law, including the commitment of Governments to human rights.

III. MODEL PROTOCOL FOR A LEGAL INVESTIGATION OF EXTRA-LEGAL,
ARBITRARY AND SUMMARY EXECUTIONS ("MINNESOTA PROTOCOL")

A. Introduction

Suspected extra-legal, arbitrary and summary executions can be investigated under established national or local laws and can lead to criminal proceedings. In some cases, however, investigative procedures may be inadequate
because of the lack of resources and expertise or because the agency assigned
to conduct the investigation may be partial. Hence, such criminal proceedings
are less likely to be brought to a successful outcome.

The following comments may enable those conducting investigations and
other parties, as appropriate, to obtain some in-depth guidance for conducting
investigations. Such guidance in a general way, has been set out in the
Principles on the Effective Prevention and Investigation of Extra-Legal,
Arbitrary and Summary Executions (see annex I, below, paragraphs 9-17). The
guidelines set forth in this proposed model protocol for a legal investigation
of extra-legal, arbitrary and summary executions are not binding. Instead,
the model protocol is meant to be illustrative of methods for carrying out the
standards enumerated in the Principles.

By definition, this model protocol cannot be exhaustive as the variety of
legal and political arrangements escapes its application. Also, investigative
techniques vary from country to country and these cannot be standardized in
the form of internationally adopted principles. Consequently, additional
comments may be relevant for the practical implementation of the Principles.

Sections B and C of this model protocol contain guidelines for the
investigation of all violent, sudden, unexpected or suspicious deaths,
including suspected extra-legal, arbitrary and summary executions. These
guidelines apply to investigations conducted by law enforcement personnel and
by members of an independent commission of inquiry.

Section D provides guidelines for establishing a special independent commission of inquiry. These guidelines are based on the experiences of several
countries that have established independent commissions to investigate alleged
arbitrary executions.

Several considerations should be taken into account when a Government
decides to establish an independent commission of inquiry. First, persons
subject to an inquiry should be guaranteed the minimum procedural safeguards
protected by international law* at all stages of the investigation. Secondly,
investigators should have the support of adequate technical and administrative
personnel, as well as access to objective, impartial legal advice to ensure
that the investigation will produce admissible evidence for later criminal
proceedings. Thirdly, investigators should receive the full scope of the
Government's resources and powers. Finally, investigators should have the
power to seek help from the international community of experts in law,
medicine and forensic sciences.

_____

*In particular, all persons must be guaranteed the due process rights set
forth in article 14 of the International Covenant on Civil and Political
Rights.

The fundamental principles of any viable investigation into the causes of death are competence, thoroughness, promptness and impartiality of the investigation, which flow from paragraphs 9 and 11 of the Principles. These elements can be adapted to any legal system and should guide all investigations of alleged extra-legal, arbitrary and summary executions.

B. Purposes of an inquiry

As set out in paragraph 9 of the Principles, the broad purpose of an inquiry is to discover the truth about the events leading to the suspicious death of a victim. To fulfil this purpose, those conducting the inquiry shall, at a minimum, seek:

(a) To identify the victim;

(b) To recover and preserve evidentiary material related to the death to aid in any potential prosecution of those responsible;

(c) To identify possible witnesses and obtain statements from them concerning the death;

(d) To determine the cause, manner, location and time of death, as well as any pattern or practice that may have brought about the death;

(e) To distinguish between natural death, accidental death, suicide and homicide;

(f) To identify and apprehend the person(s) involved in the death;

(g) To bring the suspected perpetrator(s) before a competent court established by law.

C. Procedures of an inquiry

One of the most important aspects of a thorough and impartial investigation of an extra-legal, arbitrary and summary execution is the collection and analysis of evidence. It is essential to recover and preserve physical evidence, and to interview potential witnesses so that the circumstances surrounding a suspicious death can be clarified.

1. Processing of the crime scene

Law enforcement personnel and other non-medical investigators should co-ordinate their efforts in processing the scene with those of medical personnel. Persons conducting an investigation should have access to the scene where the body was discovered and to the scene where the death may have occurred:

(a) The area around the body should be closed off. Only investigators and their staff should be allowed entry into the area;

(b) Colour photographs of the victim should be taken as these, in comparison with black and white photographs, may reveal in more detail the nature and circumstances of the victim's death;

(c) Photographs should be taken of the scene (interior and exterior) and of any other physical evidence;

(d) A record should be made of the body position and condition of the clothing;

(e) The following factors may be helpful in estimating the time of death:

(i) Temperature of the body (warm, cool, cold);

(ii) Location and degree of fixation of lividity;

(iii) Rigidity of the body;

(iv) Stage of its decomposition;

(f) Examination of the scene for blood should take place. Any samples of blood, hair, fibres and threads should be collected and preserved;

(g) If the victim appears to have been sexually assaulted, this fact should be recorded;

(h) A record should be made of any vehicles found in the area;

(i) Castings should be made and preserved of pry marks, tyre or shoe impressions, or any other impressions of an evidentiary nature;

(j) Any evidence of weapons, such as guns, projectiles, bullets and cartridge cases, should be taken and preserved. When applicable, tests for gunshot residue and trace metal detection should be performed;

(k) Any fingerprints should be located, developed, lifted and preserved;

(l) A sketch of the crime scene to scale should be made showing all relevant details of the crime, such as the location of weapons, furniture, vehicles, surrounding terrain, including the position, height and width of items, and their relationship to each other;

(m) A record of the identity of all persons at the scene should be made, including complete names, addresses and telephone numbers;

(n) Information should be obtained from scene witnesses, including those who last saw the decedent alive, when, where and under what circumstances;

(o) Any relevant papers, records or documents should be saved for evidentiary use and handwriting analysis.

2. Processing of the evidence

(a) The body must be identified by reliable witnesses and other objective methods;

(b) A report should be made detailing any observations at the scene, actions of investigators and disposition of all evidence recovered;

(c) Property forms listing all evidence should be completed;

(d) Evidence must be properly collected, handled, packaged, labelled and placed in safekeeping to prevent contamination and loss of evidence.

3. Avenues to investigation

(a) What evidence is there, if any, that the death was premeditated and intentional, rather than accidental? Is there any evidence of torture?

(b) What weapon or means was used and in what manner?

(c) How many persons were involved in the death?

(d) What other crime, if any, and the exact details thereof, was committed during or associated with the death?

(e) What was the relationship between the suspected perpetrator(s) and the victim prior to the death?

(f) Was the victim a member of any political, religious, ethnic or social group(s), and could this have been a motive for the death?

4. Personal testimony

(a) Investigators should identify and interview all potential witnesses to the crime, including:

    (i) Suspects;

    (ii) Relatives and friends of the victim;

    (iii) Persons who knew the victim;

    (iv) Individuals residing or located in the area of the crime;

    (v) Persons who knew or had knowledge of the suspects;

    (vi) Persons who may have observed either the crime, the scene, the victim or the suspects in the week prior to the execution;

    (vii) Persons having knowledge of possible motives;

(b) Interviews should take place as soon as possible and should be written and/or taped. All tapes should be transcribed and maintained;

(c) Witnesses should be interviewed individually, and assurance should be given that any possible means of protecting their safety before, during and after the proceedings will be used, if necessary.

D. Commission of inquiry

In cases where government involvement is suspected, an objective and impartial investigation may not be possible unless a special commission of inquiry is established. A commission of inquiry may also be necessary where the expertise of the investigators is called into question. This section sets out factors that give rise to a presumption of government complicity, partiality or insufficient expertise on the part of those conducting the investigation. Any one of these presumptions should trigger the creation of a special commission of inquiry. It then sets out procedures that can be used as a model for the creation and function of commissions of inquiry. The procedures were derived from the experience of major inquiries that have been mounted to investigate executions or similarly grievous cases of human rights violations.

Establishing a commission of inquiry entails defining the scope of the inquiry, appointing commission members and staff, determining the type of proceedings to be followed and selecting procedures governing those proceedings, and authorizing the commission to report on its findings and make recommendations. Each of these areas will be covered separately.

1. Factors triggering a special investigation

Factors that support a belief that the Government was involved in the execution, and that should trigger the creation of a special impartial investigation commission include:

(a) Where the political views, religious or ethnic affiliation, or social status of the victim give rise to a suspicion of government involvement or complicity in the death because of any one or combination of the following factors:

> (i) Where the victim was last seen alive in police custody or detention;

> (ii) Where the modus operandi is recognizably attributable to government-sponsored death squads;

> (iii) Where persons in the Government or associated with the Government have attempted to obstruct or delay the investigation of the execution;

> (iv) Where the physical or testimonial evidence essential to the investigation becomes unavailable.

(b) As set out in paragraph 11 of the Principles, an independent commission of inquiry or similar procedure should also be established where a routine investigation is inadequate for the following reasons:

> (i) The lack of expertise; or

> (ii) The lack of impartiality; or

> (iii) The importance of the matter; or

> (iv) The apparent existence of a pattern of abuse; or

> (v) Complaints from the family of the victim about the above inadequacies or other substantial reasons.

2. Defining the scope of the inquiry

Governments and organizations establishing commissions of inquiry need to define the scope of the inquiry by including terms of reference in their authorization. Defining the commission's terms of reference can greatly increase its success by giving legitimacy to the proceedings, assisting commission members in reaching a consensus on the scope of inquiry and providing a measure by which the commission's final report can be judged. Recommendations for defining terms of reference are as follows:

(a) They should be neutrally framed so that they do not suggest a predetermined outcome. To be neutral, terms of reference must not limit investigations in areas that might uncover government responsibility for extra-legal, arbitrary and summary executions;

(b) They should state precisely which events and issues are to be investigated and addressed in the commission's final report;

(c) They should provide flexibility in the scope of inquiry to ensure that thorough investigation by the commission is not hampered by overly restrictive or overly broad terms of reference. The necessary flexibility may be accomplished, for example by permitting the commission to amend its terms of reference as necessary. It is important, however, that the commission keep the public informed of any amendments to its charge.

3. Power of the commission

The principles set out in a general manner the powers of the commission. More specifically such a commission would need the following:

(a) To have the authority to obtain all information necessary to the inquiry, for example, for determining the cause, manner and time of death, including the authority to compel testimony under legal sanction, to order the production of documents including government and medical records, and to protect witnesses, families of the victim and other sources;

(b) To have the authority to issue a public report;

(c) To have the authority to prevent the burial or other disposal of the body until an adequate postmortem examination has been performed;

(d) To have the authority to conduct on-site visits, both at the scene where the body was discovered and at the scene where the death may have occurred;

(e) To have the authority to receive evidence from witnesses and organizations located outside the country.

4. Membership qualifications

Commission members should be chosen for their recognized impartiality, competence and independence as individuals:

Impartiality. Commission members should not be closely associated with any individual, government entity, political party or other organization potentially implicated in the execution or disappearance, or an organization or group associated with the victim, as this may damage the commission's credibility.

Competence. Commission members must be capable of evaluating and weighing evidence, and exercising sound judgement. If possible, commissions of inquiry should include individuals with expertise in law, medicine, forensic science and other specialized fields, as appropriate.

Independence. Members of the commission should have a reputation in their community for honesty and fairness.

5. Number of commissioners

The Principles do not contain a provision on the number of members of the commission, but it would not be unreasonable to note that objectivity of the investigation and commission's findings may, among other things, depend on whether it has three or more members rather than one or two. Investigations into extra-legal, arbitrary and summary executions should, in general, not be conducted by a single commissioner. A single, isolated commissioner will generally be limited in the depth of investigation he or she can conduct alone. In addition, a single commissioner will have to make controversial and important decisions without debate, and will be particularly vulnerable to governmental and other outside pressure.

6. Choosing a commission counsel

Commissions of inquiry should have impartial, expert counsel. Where the commission is investigating allegations of governmental misconduct, it would be advisable to appoint counsel outside the Ministry of Justice. The chief counsel to the commission should be insulated from political influence, as through civil service tenure, or status as a wholly independent member of the bar.

7. Choosing expert advisors

The investigation will often require expert advisors. Technical expertise in such areas as pathology, forensic science and ballistics should be available to the commission.

8. Choosing investigators

To conduct a completely impartial and thorough investigation, the commission will almost always need its own investigators to pursue leads and to develop evidence. The credibility of an inquiry will be significantly enhanced to the extent that the commission can rely on its own investigators.

9. Protection of witnesses

(a) The Government shall protect complainants, witnesses, those conducting the investigation, and their families from violence, threats of violence or any other form of intimidation;

(b) If the commission concludes that there is a reasonable fear of persecution, harassment, or harm to any witness or prospective witness, the commission may find it advisable:

   (i) To hear the evidence in camera;

   (ii) To keep the identity of the informant or witness confidential;

   (iii) To use only such evidence as will not present a risk of identifying the witness;

   (iv) To take any other appropriate measures.

10. Proceedings

It follows from general principles of criminal procedure that hearings should be conducted in public, unless in camera proceedings are necessary to protect the safety of a witness. In camera proceedings should be recorded and the closed, unpublished record kept in a known location.

Occasionally, complete secrecy may be required to encourage testimony, and the commission will want to hear witnesses privately, informally and without recording testimony.

11. Notice of inquiry

Wide notice of the establishment of a commission and the subject of the inquiry should be given. The notice should also include an invitation to submit relevant information and/or written statements to the commission, and instructions to persons wishing to testify. Notice can be disseminated through newspapers, magazines, radio, television, leaflets and posters.

12. Receipt of evidence

Power to compel evidence. As emphasized in Principle 10 (see annex I), commissions of inquiry should have the power to compel testimony and production of documents: in this context, Principle 10 refers to "the authority to oblige officials" allegedly involved in extra-legal, arbitrary and summary executions. Practically, this authority may involve the power to impose fines or sentences if the Government or individuals refuse to comply.

Use of witness statements. Commissions of inquiry should invite persons to testify or submit written statements as a first step in gathering evidence. Written statements may become an important source of evidence if their authors become afraid to testify, cannot travel to proceedings, or are otherwise unavailable.

Use of evidence from other proceedings. Commissions of inquiry should review other proceedings that could provide relevant information. For example, the commission should obtain the findings from an inquest into cause of death, conducted by a coroner or medical examiner. Such inquests generally rely on postmortem or autopsy examinations. A commission of inquiry should review the inquest and the results of the autopsy presented to the inquest to determine if they were conducted thoroughly and impartially. If the inquest and autopsy were so conducted, the coroner's findings are entitled to be given great weight.

13. Rights of parties

As mentioned in Principle 16, families of the deceased and their legal representatives shall be informed of, and have access to, any hearing and to all information relevant to the investigation, and shall be entitled to present evidence. This particular emphasis on the role of the family as a party to the proceedings implies the specially important role the family's interests play in the conduct of the investigation. However, all other interested parties should also have the opportunity at being heard. As mentioned in Principle 10, the investigative body shall be entitled to issue summons to witnesses, including the officials allegedly involved and to demand the production of evidence. All these witnesses should be permitted legal counsel if they are likely to be harmed by the inquiry, for example, when their testimony could expose them to criminal charges or civil liability. Witnesses may not be compelled to testify against themselves regarding matters unrelated to the scope of inquiry.

There should be an opportunity for the effective questioning of witnesses by the commission. Parties to the inquiry should be allowed to submit written questions to the commission.

14. Evaluation of evidence

The commission shall assess all information and evidence it receives to determine its relevance, veracity, reliability and probity. The commission should evaluate oral testimony based upon the demeanour and overall credibility of the witness. Corroboration of evidence from several sources will increase the probative value of such evidence. The reliability of hearsay evidence from several sources will increase the probative value of such evidence. The reliability of hearsay evidence must be considered carefully before the commission should accept it as fact. Testimony not tested by cross-examination must also be viewed with caution. In camera testimony preserved in a closed record or not recorded at all is often not subjected to cross-examination and therefore may be given less weight.

15. The report of the commission

As stated in Principle 17, the commission should issue a public report within a reasonable period of time. It may be added that where the commission is not unanimous in its findings, the minority commissioner(s) should file a dissenting opinion.

From the practical experience gathered, commission of inquiry reports should contain the following information:

(a) The scope of inquiry and terms of reference;

(b) The procedures and methods of evaluating evidence;

(c) A list of all witnesses who have testified, except for those whose identities are withheld for protection and who have testified in camera, and exhibits received in evidence;

(d) The time and place of each sitting (this might be annexed to the report);

(e) The background to the inquiry such as relevant social, political and economic conditions;

(f) The specific events that occurred and the evidence upon which such findings are based;

(g) The law upon which the commission relied;

(h) The commission's conclusions based upon applicable law and findings of fact;

(i) Recommendations based upon the findings of the commission.

16. Response of the Government

The Government should either reply publicly to the commission's report or should indicate what steps it intends to take in response to the report.

IV. MODEL AUTOPSY PROTOCOL

A. Introduction

Difficult or sensitive cases should ideally be the responsibility of an objective, experienced, well-equipped and well-trained prosector (the person performing the autopsy and preparing the written report) who is separate from any potentially involved political organization or entity. Unfortunately, this ideal is often unattainable. This proposed model autopsy protocol includes a comprehensive checklist of the steps in a basic forensic postmortem examination that should be followed to the extent possible given the resources available. Use of this autopsy protocol will permit early and final resolution of potentially controversial cases and will thwart the speculation and innuendo that are fueled by unanswered, partially answered or poorly answered questions in the investigation of an apparently suspicious death.

This model autopsy protocol is intended to have several applications and may be of value to the following categories of individuals:

(a) Experienced forensic pathologists may follow this model autopsy protocol to ensure a systematic examination and to facilitate meaningful positive or negative criticism by later observers. While trained pathologists may justifiably abridge certain aspects of the postmortem examination or written descriptions of their findings in routine cases, abridged examinations or reports are never appropriate in potentially controversial cases. Rather, a systematic and comprehensive examination and report are required to prevent the omission or loss of important details;

(b) General pathologists or other physicians who have not been trained in forensic pathology but are familiar with basic postmortem examination techniques may supplement their customary autopsy procedures with this model autopsy protocol. It may also alert them to situations in which they should seek consultation, as written material cannot replace the knowledge gained through experience;

(c) Independent consultants whose expertise has been requested in observing, performing or reviewing an autopsy may cite this model autopsy protocol and its proposed minimum criteria as a basis for their actions or opinions;

(d) Governmental authorities, international political organizations, law enforcement agencies, families or friends of decedents, or representatives of potential defendants charged with responsibility for a death may use this model autopsy protocol to establish appropriate procedures for the postmortem examination prior to its performance;

(e) Historians, journalists, attorneys, judges, other physicians and representatives of the public may also use this model autopsy protocol as a benchmark for evaluating an autopsy and its findings;

(f) Governments or individuals who are attempting either to establish or upgrade their medicolegal system for investigating deaths may use this model autopsy protocol as a guideline, representing the procedures and goals to be incorporated into an ideal medicolegal system.

While performing any medicolegal death investigation, the prosector should collect information that will establish the identity of the deceased, the time and place of death, the cause of death, and the manner or mode of death (homicide, suicide, accident or natural).

It is of the utmost importance that an autopsy performed following a controversial death be thorough in scope. The documentation and recording of the autopsy findings should be equally thorough so as to permit meaningful use of the autopsy results (see annex II, below). It is important to have as few omissions or discrepancies as possible, as proponents of different interpretations of a case may take advantage of any perceived shortcomings in the investigation. An autopsy performed in a controversial death should meet certain minimum criteria if the autopsy report is to be proffered as meaningful or conclusive by the prosector, the autopsy's sponsoring agency or governmental unit, or anyone else attempting to make use of such an autopsy's findings or conclusions.

This model autopsy protocol is designed to be used in diverse situations. Resources such as autopsy rooms, X-ray equipment or adequately trained personnel are not available everywhere. Forensic pathologists must operate under widely divergent political systems. In addition, social and religious customs vary widely throughout the world; an autopsy is an expected and routine procedure in some areas, while it is abhorred in others. A prosector, therefore, may not always be able to follow all of the steps in this protocol when performing autopsies. Variation from this protocol may be inevitable or even preferable in some cases. It is suggested, however, that any major deviations, with the supporting reasons, should be noted.

It is important that the body should be made available to the prosector for a minimum of 12 hours in order to assure an adequate and unhurried examination. Unrealistic limits or conditions are occasionally placed upon the prosector with respect to the length of time permitted for the examination or the circumstances under which an examination is allowed. When conditions are imposed, the prosector should be able to refuse to perform a compromised examination and should prepare a report explaining this position. Such a refusal should not be interpreted as indicating that an examination was unnecessary or inappropriate. If the prosector decides to proceed with the examination notwithstanding difficult conditions or circumstances, he or she should include in the autopsy report an explanation of the limitations or impediments.

Certain steps in this model autopsy protocol have been emphasized by the use of **boldface type**. These represent the most essential elements of the protocol.

B. Proposed model autopsy protocol

1. Scene investigation

The prosector(s) and medical investigators should have the right of access to the scene where the body is found. **The medical personnel should be notified immediately to assure that no alteration of the body has occurred. If access to the scene was denied, if the body was altered or if information was withheld, this should be stated in the prosector's report.**

A system for co-ordination between the medical and non-medical investigators (e.g. law enforcement agencies) should be established. This should address such issues as how the prosector will be notified and who will be in charge of the scene. Obtaining certain types of evidence is often the role of the non-medical investigators, but the medical investigators who have access to the body at the scene of death should perform the following steps:

(a) **Photograph the body as it is found** and after it has been moved;

(b) **Record the body position and condition, including body warmth or coolness, lividity and rigidity;**

(c) Protect the deceased's hands, e.g. with paper bags;

(d) Note the ambient temperature. In cases where the time of death is an issue, rectal temperature should be recorded and any insects present should be collected for forensic entomological study. Which procedure is applicable will depend on the length of the apparent postmortem interval;

(e) Examine the scene for blood, as this may be useful in identifying suspects;

(f) Record the identities of all persons at the scene;

(g) Obtain information from scene witnesses, including those who last saw the decedent alive, and when, where and under what circumstances. Interview any emergency medical personnel who may have had contact with the body;

(h) **Obtain identification of the body** and other pertinent information from friends or relatives. Obtain the deceased's medical history from his or her physician(s) and hospital charts, including any previous surgery, alcohol or drug use, suicide attempts and habits;

(i) Place the body in a body pouch or its equivalent. Save this pouch after the body has been removed from it;

(j) **Store the body in a secure refrigerated location so that tampering with the body and its evidence cannot occur;**

(k) Make sure that projectiles, guns, knives and other weapons are available for examination by the responsible medical personnel;

(1) If the decedent was hospitalized prior to death, obtain admission or blood specimens and any X-rays, and review and summarize hospital records;

(m) Before beginning the autopsy, become familiar with the types of torture or violence that are prevalent in that country or locale (see annex III).

2. Autopsy

The following Protocol should be followed during the autopsy:

(a) **Record the date, starting and finishing times, and place of the autopsy** (a complex autopsy may take as long as an entire working day);

(b) **Record the name(s) of the prosector(s), the participating assistant(s), and all other persons present during the autopsy,** including the medical and/or scientific degrees and professional, political or administrative affiliations(s) of each. Each person's role in the autopsy should be indicated, and one person should be designated as the principal prosector who will have the authority to direct the performance of the autopsy. Observers and other team members are subject to direction by, and should not interfere with, the principal prosector. The time(s) during the autopsy when each person is present should be included. The use of a "sign-in" sheet is recommended;

(c) **Adequate photographs are crucial** for thorough documentation of autopsy findings:

(i) Photographs should be in colour (transparency or negative/print), in focus, adequately illuminated, and taken by a professional or good quality camera. Each photograph should contain a ruled reference scale, an identifying case name or number, and a sample of standard grey. A description of the camera (including the lens "f-number" and focal length), film and the lighting system must be included in the autopsy report. If more than one camera is utilized, the identifying information should be recorded for each. Photographs should also include information indicating which camera took each picture, if more than one camera is used. The identity of the person taking the photographs should be recorded;

(ii) Serial photographs reflecting the course of the external examination must be included. Photograph the body prior to and following undressing, washing or cleaning and shaving;

(iii) Supplement close-up photographs with distant and/or immediate range photographs to permit orientation and identification of the close-up photographs;

(iv) Photographs should be comprehensive in scope and must confirm the presence of all demonstrable signs of injury or disease commented upon in the autopsy report;

(v) Identifying facial features should be portrayed (after washing or cleaning the body), with photographs of a full frontal aspect of the face, and right and left profiles of the face with hair in normal position and with hair retracted, if necessary, to reveal the ears;

(d) **Radiograph the body** before it is removed from its pouch or wrappings. X-rays should be repeated both before and after undressing the body. Fluoroscopy may also be performed. **Photograph all X-ray films;**

(i) **Obtain dental X-rays,** even if identification has been established in other ways;

(ii) **Document any skeletal system injury by X-ray.** Skeletal X-rays may also record anatomic defects or surgical procedures. Check especially for fractures of the fingers, toes and other bones in the hands and feet. Skeletal X-rays may also aid in the identification of the deceased, by detecting identifying characteristics, estimating age and height, and determining sex and race. Frontal sinus films should also be taken, as these can be particularly useful for identification purposes;

(iii) Take X-rays in gunshot cases to aid in locating the projectile(s). Recover, photograph and save any projectile or major projectile fragment that is seen on an X-ray. Other radio-opaque objects (**pacemakers, artificial joints or valves, knife fragments etc.**) documented with X-rays should also be removed, photographed and saved;

(iv) Skeletal X-rays are essential in children **to assist in determining age and developmental status;**

(e) Before the clothing is removed, examine the body and the clothing. **Photograph the clothed body.** Record any jewellery present;

(f) The **clothing** should be carefully removed over a clean sheet or body pouch. Let the clothing dry if it is bloody or wet. Describe the clothing that is removed and **label it in a permanent fashion. Either place the clothes in the custody of a responsible person or keep them, as they may be useful as evidence or for identification;**

(g) The external examination, focusing on a search for external evidence of injury is, in most cases, the most important portion of the autopsy;

    (i)   **Photograph all surfaces – 100 per cent of the body area.** Take **good quality, well-focused, colour photographs with adequate illumination;**

    (ii)   Describe and document the means used to make the identification. Examine the body and record the deceased's apparent age, length, weight, sex, head hair style and length, nutritional status, muscular development and colour of skin, eyes and hair (head, facial and body);

    (iii)   In children, measure also the head circumference, crown-rump length and crown-heel length;

    (iv)   Record the degree, location and fixation of rigor and livor mortis;

    (v)   Note body warmth or coolness and state of preservation; **note any decomposition changes, such as skin slippage. Evaluate the general condition of the body and note adipocere formation, maggots, eggs or anything else that suggests the time or place of death;**

    (vi)   With all injuries, record the size, shape, pattern, location (related to obvious anatomic landmarks), colour, course, direction, depth and structure involved. **Attempt to distinguish injuries resulting from therapeutic measures from those unrelated to medical treatment.** In the description of projectile wounds, note the presence or absence of soot, gunpowder, or singeing. **If gunshot residue is present, document it photographically and save it for analysis. Attempt to determine whether the gunshot wound is an entry or exit wound. If an entry wound is present and no exit wound is seen, the projectile must be found and saved or accounted for. Excise wound tract tissue samples for microscopic examination. Tape together the edges of knife wounds to assess the blade size and characteristics;**

    (vii)   **Photograph all injuries,** taking two colour pictures of each, labelled with the autopsy identification number on a scale that is oriented parallel or perpendicular to the injury. Shave hair where necessary to clarify an injury, and take photographs before and after shaving. Save all hair removed from the site of the injury. Take photographs before and after washing the site of any injury. Wash the body only after any blood or material that may have come from an assailant has been collected and saved;

(viii)   Examine the skin. Note and photograph any scars, areas of
         keloid formation, tattoos, prominent moles, areas of increased
         or decreased pigmentation, and anything distinctive or unique
         such as birthmarks. Note any bruises and incise them for
         delineation of their extent. Excise them for microscopic exam-
         ination. The head and genital area should be checked with
         special care. **Note any injection sites or puncture wounds**
         and excise them to use for toxicological evaluation. **Note any
         abrasions** and excise them; microscopic sections may be useful
         for attempting to date the time of injury. **Note any bite
         marks;** these should be photographed to record the dental
         pattern, swabbed for saliva testing (before the body is washed)
         and excised for microscopic examination. Bite marks should also
         be analysed by a forensic odontologist, if possible. **Note any
         burn marks** and attempt to determine the cause (burning rubber,
         a cigarette, electricity, a blowtorch, acid, hot oil etc.).
         Excise any suspicious areas for microscopic examination, as it
         may be possible to distinguish microscopically between burns
         caused by electricity and those caused by heat;

 (ix)   **Identify and label any foreign object that is recovered,**
         including its relation to specific injuries. Do not scratch
         the sides or tip of any projectiles. **Photograph each projec-
         tile and large projectile fragment with an identifying label,
         and then place each in a sealed, padded and labelled container**
         in order to maintain the chain of custody;

  (x)   Collect a blood specimen **of at least 50 cc from a subclavian
         or femoral vessel;**

 (xi)   Examine the head and external scalp, **bearing in mind that
         injuries may be hidden by the hair. Shave hair where necessary.**
         Check for fleas and lice, as these may indicate unsanitary con-
         ditions prior to death. **Note any alopecia as this may be caused
         by malnutrition, heavy metals (e.g. thallium), drugs or trac-
         tion. Pull, do not cut, 20 representative head hairs and save
         them, as hair may also be useful for detecting some drugs and
         poisons;**

(xii)   **Examine the teeth and note their condition.** Record any that
         are absent, loose or damaged, and record all dental work
         (restorations, fillings etc.), using a dental identification
         system to identify each tooth. Check the gums for periodontal
         disease. Photograph dentures, if any, and save them if the
         decedent's identity is unknown. Remove the mandible and
         maxilla if necessary for identification. **Check the inside of
         the mouth and note any evidence of trauma, injection sites,
         needle marks or biting of the lips, cheeks or tongue.** Note
         any articles or substances in the mouth. In cases of suspected
         sexual assault, save oral fluid or get a swab for spermatozoa
         and acid phosphatase evaluation. (Swabs taken at the tooth-gum
         junction and samples from between the teeth provide the best
         specimens for identifying spermatozoa.) Also take swabs from
         the oral cavity for seminal fluid typing. Dry the swabs quickly
         with cool, blown air if possible, and preserve them in clean
         plain paper envelopes. If rigor mortis prevents an adequate
         examination, the masseter muscles may be cut to permit better
         exposure;

(xiii) **Examine the face** and note if it is cyanotic or if petechiae are present;

       a. **Examine the eyes** and view the conjunctiva of both the globes and the eyelids. Note any petechiae in the upper or lower eyelids. Note any scleral icterus. Save contact lenses, if any are present. **Collect at least 1 ml of vitreous humor from each eye;**

       b. **Examine the nose and ears** and note any evidence of trauma, haemorrhage or other abnormalities. Examine the tympanic membranes;

(xiv) **Examine the neck** externally on all aspects and note any contusions, abrasions or petechiae. Describe and document injury patterns to differentiate manual, ligature and hanging strangulation. Examine the neck at the conclusion of the autopsy, when the blood has drained out of the area and the tissues are dry;

(xv) **Examine all surfaces of the extremities: arms, forearms, wrists, hands, legs and feet,** and note any "defence" wounds. **Dissect and describe any injuries.** Note any bruises about the wrists or ankles that may suggest restraints such as hand- cuffs or suspension. Examine the medial and lateral surfaces of the fingers, the anterior forearms and the backs of the knees for bruises;

(xvi) Note any broken or missing fingernails. Note any gunpowder residue on the hands, document photographically and save it for analysis. **Take fingerprints in all cases.** If the decedent's identity is unknown and fingerprints cannot be obtained, remove the "glove" of the skin, if present. Save the fingers if no other means of obtaining fingerprints is possible. Save finger- nail clippings and any under-nail tissue (nail scrapings). Examine the fingernail and toenail beds for evidence of objects having been pushed beneath the nails. Nails can be removed by dissecting the lateral margins and proximal base, and then the undersurface of the nails can be inspected. If this is done, the hands must be photographed before and after the nails are removed. **Carefully examine the soles of the feet,** noting any evidence of beating. Incise the soles to delineate the extent of any injuries. Examine the palms and knees, looking especially for glass shards or lacerations;

(xvii) **Examine the external genitalia** and note the presence of any foreign material or semen. Note the size, location and number of any abrasions or contusions. Note any injury to the inner thighs or peri-anal area. Look for peri-anal burns;

(xviii) In cases of suspected sexual assault, examine all potentially involved orifices. **A speculum should be used to examine the vaginal walls. Collect foreign hair by combing the pubic hair. Pull and save at least 20 of the deceased's own pubic hairs, including roots. Aspirate fluid from the vagina and/or rectum for acid phosphatase, blood group and spermatozoa evaluation. Take swabs from the same areas for seminal fluid typing. Dry the swabs quickly with cool, blown air if possible, and preserve them in clean plain paper envelopes;**

(xix) The length of the back, the buttocks and extremities including wrists and ankles must be systematically incised to look for deep injuries. The shoulders, elbows, hips and knee joints must also be incised to look for ligamentous injury;

(h) The internal examination for internal evidence of injury should clarify and augment the external examination;

(i) Be systematic in the internal examination. **Perform the examination either by body regions or by systems, including the cardiovascular, respiratory, biliary, gastrointestinal, reticuloendothelial, genitourinary, endocrine, musculoskeletal, and central nervous systems.** Record the weight, size, shape, colour and consistency of each organ, and note any neoplasia, inflammation, anomalies, haemorrhage, ischemia, infarcts, surgical procedures or injuries. Take sections of normal and any abnormal areas of each organ for microscopic examination. **Take samples of any fractured bones for radiographic and microscopic estimation of the age of the fracture;**

(ii) **Examine the chest.** Note any abnormalities of the breasts. Record any rib fractures, noting whether cardiopulmonary resuscitation was attempted. Before opening, check for pneumothoraces. Record the thickness of subcutaneous fat. Immediately after opening the chest, evaluate the pleural cavities and the pericardial sac for the presence of blood or other fluid, and describe and quantify any fluid present. Save any fluid present until foreign objects are accounted for. Note the presence of air embolism, characterized by frothy blood within the right atrium and right ventricle. **Trace any injuries before removing the organs.** If blood is not available at other sites, collect a sample directly from the heart. **Examine the heart,** noting degree and location of coronary artery disease or other abnormalities. **Examine the lungs,** noting any abnormalities;

(iii) **Examine the abdomen** and record the amount of subcutaneous fat. Retain 50 grams of adipose tissue for toxicological evaluation. Note the interrelationships of the organs. **Trace any injuries before removing the organs.** Note any fluid or blood present in the peritoneal cavity, and save it until foreign objects are accounted for. **Save all urine** and bile for toxicologic examination;

(iv) Remove, examine and record the quantitative information on the liver, spleen, pancreas, kidneys and adrenal glands. Save at least 150 grams each of kidney and liver **for toxicological** evaluation. Remove the gastrointestinal tract and examine the contents. Note any food present and its degree of digestion. **Save the contents of the stomach.** If a more detailed toxicological evaluation is desired, the contents of other regions of the gastrointestinal tract may be saved. **Examine the rectum and anus** for burns, lacerations or other injuries. Locate and retain any foreign bodies present. **Examine the aorta, inferior vena cava and iliac vessels;**

(v)   **Examine the organs in the pelvis,** including ovaries,
      fallopian tubes, uterus, vagina, testes, prostate gland,
      seminal vesicles, urethra and urinary bladder. **Trace any
      injuries before removing the organs.** Remove these organs
      carefully so as not to injure them artifactually. Note any
      evidence of previous or current pregnancy, miscarriage or
      delivery. Save any foreign objects within the cervix, uterus,
      vagina, urethra or rectum;

(vi) **Palpate the head** and examine the external and internal
      surfaces of the scalp, noting any trauma or haemorrhage. **Note
      any skull fractures.** Remove the calvarium carefully and note
      epidural and subdural haematomas. Quantify, date and save any
      haematomas that are present. Remove the dura to examine the
      internal surface of the skull for fractures. **Remove the
      brain** and note any abnormalities. **Dissect and describe any
      injuries.** Cerebral cortical atrophy, whether focal or
      generalized, should be specifically commented upon;

(vii) Evaluate the cerebral vessels. Save at least 150 grams of
      cerebral tissue for toxicological evaluation. Submerge the
      brain in fixative prior to examination, if this is indicated;

(viii) **Examine the neck after the heart and brain have been removed
      and the neck vessels have been drained. Remove the neck
      organs,** taking care not to fracture the hyoid bone. **Dissect
      and describe any injuries.** Check the mucosa of the larynx,
      pyriform sinuses and esophagus, and note any petechiae, edema
      or burns caused by corrosive substances. Note any articles or
      substances within the lumina of these structures. Examine the
      thyroid gland. Separate and examine the parathyroid glands, if
      they are readily identifiable;

(ix) Dissect the neck muscles, noting any haemorrhage. Remove all
      organs, including the tongue. Dissect the muscles from the
      bones and note any fractures of the hyoid bone or thyroid or
      cricoid cartilages;

(x)   **Examine the cervical, thoracic and lumbar spine.** Examine the
      vertebrae from their anterior aspects and note any fractures,
      dislocations, compressions or haemorrhages. Examine the
      vertebral bodies. Cerebrospinal fluid may be obtained if
      additional toxicological evaluation is indicated;

(xi) **In cases in which spinal injury is suspected, dissect and
      describe the spinal cord.** Examine the cervical spine
      anteriorly and note any haemorrhage in the paravertebral
      muscles. The posterior approach is best for evaluating high
      cervical injuries. Open the spinal canal and remove the spinal
      cord. Make transverse sections every 0.5 cm and note any
      abnormalities;

(i) After the autopsy has been completed, **record which specimens have
been saved.** Label all specimens with the name of the deceased, the autopsy
identification number, the date and time of collection, the name of the
prosector and the contents. **Carefully preserve all evidence and record the
chain of custody with appropriate release forms;**

(i) Perform appropriate toxicologic tests and retain portions of the tested samples to permit retesting;

    a. Tissues: 150 grams of liver and kidney should be saved routinely. Brain, hair and adipose tissue may be saved for additional studies in cases where drugs, poisons or other toxic substances are suspected;

    b. Fluids: 50 cc (if possible) of blood (spin and save serum in all or some of the tubes), all available urine, vitreous humor and stomach contents should be saved routinely. Bile, regional gastrointestinal tract contents and cerebrospinal fluid should be saved in cases where drugs, poisons or toxic substances are suspected. Oral, vaginal and rectal fluid should be saved in cases of suspected sexual assault;

(ii) Representative samples of all major organs, including areas of normal and any abnormal tissue, should be processed histolog- ically and stained with hematoxylin and eosin (and other stains as indicated). The slides, wet tissue and paraffin blocks should be kept indefinitely;

(iii) Evidence that must be saved includes:

    a. All foreign objects, including projectiles, projectile fragments, pellets, knives and fibres. **Projectiles must be subjected to ballistic analysis;**

    b. All clothes and personal effects of the deceased, worn by or in the possession of the deceased at the time of death;

    c. Fingernails and under nail scrapings;

    d. Hair, foreign and pubic, in cases of suspected sexual assault;

    e. Head hair, in cases where the place of death or location of the body prior to its discovery may be an issue;

(j) After the autopsy, all unretained organs should be replaced in the body, and the body should be well embalmed to facilitate a second autopsy in case one is desired at some future point;

(k) The written autopsy report should address those items that are emphasized in boldface type in the protocol. At the end of the autopsy report should be a summary of the findings and the cause of death. This should include the prosector's comments attributing any injuries to external trauma, therapeutic efforts, postmortem change, or other causes. A full report should be given to the appropriate authorities and to the deceased's family.

V. MODEL PROTOCOL FOR DISINTERMENT AND ANALYSIS OF SKELETAL REMAINS

A. Introduction

This proposed model protocol for the disinterment and analysis of skeletal remains includes a comprehensive checklist of the steps in a basic forensic examination. The objectives of an anthropological investigation are the same as those of a medicolegal investigation of a recently deceased person. The anthropologist must collect information that will establish the identity of the deceased, the time and place of death, the cause of death and the manner or mode of death (homicide, suicide, accident or natural). The approach of the anthropologist differs, however, because of the nature of the material to be examined. Typically, a prosector is required to examine a body, whereas an anthropologist is required to examine a skeleton. The prosector focuses on information obtained from soft tissues, whereas the anthropologist focuses on information from hard tissues. Since decomposition is a continuous process, the work of both specialists can overlap. An anthropologist may examine a fresh body when bone is exposed or when bone trauma is a factor. An experienced prosector may be required when mummified tissues are present. In some circumstances, use of both this protocol and the model autopsy protocol may be necessary to yield the maximum information. The degree of decomposition of the body will dictate the type of investigation and, therefore, the protocol(s) to be followed.

The questions addressed by the anthropologist differ from those pursued in a typical autopsy. The anthropological investigation invests more time and attention to basic questions such as the following:

(a) Are the remains human?

(b) Do they represent a single individual or several?

(c) What was the decedent's sex, race, stature, body weight, handedness and physique?

(d) Are there any skeletal traits or anomalies that could serve to positively identify the decedent?

The time, cause and manner of death are also addressed by the anthropologist, but the margin of error is usually greater than that which can be achieved by an autopsy shortly after death.

This model protocol may be of use in many diverse situations. Its application may be affected, however, by poor conditions, inadequate financial resources or lack of time. Variation from the protocol may be inevitable or even preferable in some cases. It is suggested, however, that any major deviations, with the supporting reasons, should be noted in the final report.

B. Proposed model skeletal analysis protocol

1. Scene investigation

A burial recovery should be handled with the same exacting care given to a crime-scene search. Efforts should be co-ordinated between the principal investigator and the consulting physical anthropologist or archaeologist. Human remains are frequently exhumed by law enforcement officers or cemetery workers unskilled in the techniques of forensic anthropology. Valuable information may be lost in this manner and false information is sometimes generated. Disinterment by untrained persons should be prohibited. The consulting anthropologist should be present to conduct or supervise the disinterment. Specific problems and procedures accompany the excavation of each type of burial. The amount of information obtained from the excavation depends on knowledge of the burial situation and judgement based on experience. The final report should include a rationale for the excavation procedure.

The following procedure should be followed during disinterment:

(a) Record the date, location, starting and finishing times of the disinterment, and the names of all workers;

(b) Record the information in narrative form, supplemented by sketches and photographs;

(c) Photograph the work area from the same perspective before work begins and after it ends every day to document any disturbance not related to the official procedure;

(d) In some cases, it is necessary to first locate the grave within a given area. There are numerous methods of locating graves, depending on the age of the grave:

(i) An experienced archaeologist may recognize clues such as changes in surface contour and variation in local vegetation;

(ii) A metal probe can be used to locate the less compact soil characteristics of grave fill;

(iii) The area to be explored can be cleared and the top soil scraped away with a flat shovel. Graves appear darker than the surrounding ground because the darker topsoil has mixed with the lighter subsoil in the grave fill. Sometimes a light spraying of the surface with water may enhance a grave's outline;

(e) Classify the burial as follows:

(i) Individual or commingled. A grave may contain the remains of one person buried alone, or it may contain the commingled remains of two or more persons buried either at the same time or over a period of time;

(ii) Isolated or adjacent. An isolated grave is separate from other graves and can be excavated without concern about encroaching upon another grave. Adjacent graves, such as in a crowded cemetery, require a different excavation technique because the wall of one grave is also the wall of another grave;

(iii) Primary or secondary. A primary grave is the grave in which the deceased is first placed. If the remains are then removed and reburied, the grave is considered to be secondary;

(iv) Undisturbed or disturbed. An undisturbed burial is unchanged (except by natural processes) since the time of primary burial. A disturbed burial is one that has been altered by human intervention after the time of primary burial. All secondary burials are considered to be disturbed; archaeological methods can be used to detect a disturbance in a primary burial;

(f) Assign an unambiguous number to the burial. If an adequate numbering system is not already in effect, the anthropologist should devise a system;

(g) Establish a datum point, then block and map the burial site using an appropriate-sized grid and standard archaeological techniques. In some cases, it may be adequate simply to measure the depth of the grave from the surface to the skull and from the surface to the feet. Associated material can then be recorded in terms of their position relative to the skeleton;

(h) Remove the overburden of earth, screening the dirt for associated materials. Record the level (depth) and relative co-ordinates of any such findings. The type of burial, especially whether primary or secondary, influences the care and attention that needs to be given to this step. Associated materials located at a secondary burial site are unlikely to reveal the circumstances of the primary burial but may provide information on events that have occurred after that burial;

(i) Search for items such as bullets or jewellery, for which a metal detector can be useful, particularly in the levels immediately above and below the level of the remains;

(j) Circumscribe the body, when the level of the burial is located, and, when possible, open the burial pit to a minimum of 30 cm on all sides of the body;

(k) Pedestal the burial by digging on all sides to the lowest level of the body (approximately 30 cm). Also pedestal any associated artifacts;

(l) Expose the remains with the use of a soft brush or whisk broom. Do not use a brush on fabric, as it may destroy fibre evidence. Examine the soil found around the skull for hair. Place this soil in a bag for laboratory study. Patience is invaluable at this time. The remains may be fragile, and interrelationships of elements are important and may be easily disrupted. Damage can seriously reduce the amount of information available for analysis;

(m) Photograph and map the remains _in situ_. All photographs should include an identification number, the date, a scale and an indication of magnetic north;

   (i) First photograph the entire burial, then focus on significant details so that their relation to the whole can be easily visualized;

   (ii) Anything that seems unusual or remarkable should be photographed at close range. Careful attention should be given to evidence of trauma or pathological change, either recent or healed;

   (iii) Photograph and map all associated materials (clothes, hair, coffin, artifacts, bullets, casings etc.). The map should include a rough sketch of the skeleton as well as any associated materials;

(n) Before displacing anything, measure the individual:

   (i) Measure the total length of the remains and record the terminal points of the measurement, e.g. apex to plantar surface of calcaneus (note: This is not a stature measurement);

(ii) If the skeleton is so fragile that it may break when lifted,
        measure as much as possible before removing it from the ground;

(o) Remove all elements and place them in bags or boxes, taking care to
avoid damage. Number, date and initial every container;

(p) Excavate and screen the level of soil immediately under the burial.
A level of "sterile" (artifact-free) soil should be located before ceasing
excavation and beginning to backfill.

2. Laboratory analysis of skeletal remains

The following protocol should be followed during the laboratory analysis
of the skeletal remains:

(a) Record the date, location, starting and finishing times of the
skeletal analysis, and the names of all workers;

(b) Radiograph all skeletal elements before any further cleaning:

(i) Obtain bite-wing, apical and panoramic dental X-rays, if
      possible;

(ii) The entire skeleton should be X-rayed. Special attention
      should be directed to fractures, developmental anomalies and
      the effects of surgical procedures. Frontal sinus films should
      be included for identification purposes;

(c) Retain some bones in their original state; two lumbar vertebrae
should be adequate. Rinse the rest of the bones clean but do not soak or scrub
them. Allow the bones to dry;

(d) Lay out the entire skeleton in a systematic way:

(i) Distinguish left from right;

(ii) Inventory every bone and record on a skeletal chart;

(iii) Inventory the teeth and record on a dental chart. Note broken,
        carious, restored and missing teeth;

(iv) Photograph the entire skeleton in one frame. All photographs
       should contain an identification number and scale;

(e) If more than one individual is to be analysed, and especially if
there is any chance that comparisons will be made between individuals, number
every element with indelible ink before any other work is begun;

(f) Record the condition of the remains, e.g. fully intact and solid,
eroding and friable, charred or cremated;

(g) Preliminary identification:

(i) Determine age, sex, race and stature;

(ii) Record the reasons for each conclusion (e.g. sex identity based
       on skull and femoral head);

   (iii) Photograph all evidence supporting these conclusions;

(h) Individual identification:

    (i) Search for evidence of handedness, pathological change, trauma and developmental anomalies;

   (ii) Record the reasons for each conclusion;

  (iii) Photograph all evidence supporting these conclusions;

(i) Attempt to distinguish injuries resulting from therapeutic measures from those unrelated to medical treatment. Photograph all injuries:

    (i) Examine the hyoid bone for cracks or breaks;

   (ii) Examine the thyroid cartilage for damage;

  (iii) Each bone should be examined for evidence of contact with metal. The superior or inferior edges of the ribs require particular scrutiny. A dissecting microscope is useful;

(j) If the remains are to be reburied before obtaining an identification, retain the following samples for further analysis:

    (i) A mid-shaft cross-section from either femur, 2 cm or more in height;

   (ii) A mid-shaft cross-section from either fibula, 2 cm or more in height;

  (iii) A 4-cm section from the sternal end of a rib (sixth, if possible);

  (iv) A tooth (preferably a mandibular incisor) that was vital at the time of death;

   (v) Sever molar teeth for possible later deoxyribonucleic acid fingerprinting for identification;

  (vi) A cast of the skull for possible facial reconstruction;

 (vii) Record what samples have been saved, and label all samples with the identification number, date and name of the person who removed the sample.

3. **Final report**

The following steps should be taken in the preparation of a final report:

(a) Prepare a full report of all procedures and results;

(b) Include a short summary of the conclusions;

(c) Sign and date the report.

4. Repository for evidence

In cases where the body cannot be identified, the exhumed remains or other evidence should be preserved for a reasonable time. A repository should be established to hold the bodies for 5-10 years in case they can be identified at a later time.

Notes

1/ Advisory Services and Technical Assistance in the Field of Human Rights, Human Rights Fact Sheet No. 3 (Geneva, United Nations Centre for Human Rights, 1988); Summary or Arbitrary Executions, Human Rights Fact Sheet No.11 (Geneva, United Nations Centre for Human Rights, 1990); see, also, The Teaching of Human Rights: Proceedings of the International Congress on the Teaching of Human Rights, Vienna, 12-16 September 1978 (Paris, United Nations Organization for Education, Science and Culture, 1980).

2/ Methods of Combating Torture, Human Rights Fact Sheet No. 4 (Geneva, United Nations Centre for Human Rights, 1987), pp. 7-9 and 10-12. See also Laurence Boisson de Chazoumes and others, Practical Guide to the International Procedures Relative to Complaint and Appeals Against Acts of Torture, Disappearances and Other Inhuman or Degrading Treatment (Geneva, World Organization Against Torture, 1988).

3/ See D. O'Donnell, Proteccion internacional de los derechos humanos, 2. ed. (Lima, Comisión Andina de Juristas, 1989); and N. S. Rodley, The Treatment of Prisoners under International Law (Oxford, Clarendon Press, 1987), pp. 144-164 and B. G. Ramcharan, "The Concept and Dimensions of the Right to Life", The Right to Life in International Law (Dordrecht, Martinus Nijhoff Publishers, 1985), pp. 1-32.

4/ Report of the Human Rights Committee (Official Records of the General Assembly, Thirty-seventh session, Supplement No. 40) (A/37/40), annex X. See also M. Novak, UNO-Pakt über bürgerliche und politische Rechte und Fakultativprotokoll; CCPR-Kommentar (Kehl am Rhein, N.P. Engel Verlag, 1989), pp. 111-132; and F. Newman and D. Weissbrodt, International Human Rights: Law, Policy, and Process (Cincinnati, Ohio, Anderson, 1990).

5/ Report of the Human Rights Committee (Official Records of the General Assembly, Fortieth session, Supplement No. 40) (A/40/40), annex X. See, also, Enforced or Voluntary Disappearances, Human Rights Fact Sheet No. 6 (Geneva, United Nations Centre for Human Rights, 1988).

6/ Statement submitted by the International Commission of Jurists, a non-governmental organization in consultative status with the Economic and Social Council, category II, and the International Human Rights Internship Program, a non-governmental organization in consultative status with the Economic and Social Council, roster (E/AC.57/1988/NGO.4).

7/ Sixth United Nations Congress on the Prevention of Crime and the Treatment of Offenders, Caracas, Venezuela, 25 August-5 September 1980; Report prepared by the Secretariat (United Nations publication, Sales No. E.81.IV.4), chap. I, sect. A.

8/ Seventh United Nations Congress on the Prevention of Crime and the Treatment of Offenders, Milan, 26 August-6 September 1985: Report prepared by the Secretariat (United Nations publication, Sales No. E.86.IV.1), chap. I, sect. E.

9/ International Labour Office, Governing Body, Two Hundred and Eighteenth Report of the Committee on Freedom of Association (GB.221/6/16), para. 390(c).

10/ Annual report of the Inter-American Commission on Human Rights 1981-1982, OAS doc. OEA/Ser.L/V/II.57, doc. 6, rev.1 (Washington, D.C., 1982), p. 36.

11/ For a general overview of the question see E. R. Zafaroni, "The right to life and Latin American penal systems", The Annals of the American Academy of Political and Social Science, Marvin E. Wolfgang, ed., vol. 506, November 1989, pp. 57-67.

12/ See, Inter-American Court H.R., Velasquez Rodriguez Case, Judgment of July 29, 1988, series C, No. 4; Inter-American Court H.R., Godinez Cruz Case, Judgment of January 20, 1989, series C, No. 5.

13/ Cyprus v. Turkey, Apps. No. 6780/74 and 6950/75, Decision of 17 July 1976, European Human Rights Reports, 482 (1982).

14/ J. L. Thomsen and others, "Amnesty International and the forensic sciences", American Journal for Medical Pathology, vol. 5, No. 4 (December 1984), pp. 305-311.

Annex I

PRINCIPLES ON THE EFFECTIVE PREVENTION AND INVESTIGATION
OF EXTRA-LEGAL, ARBITRARY AND SUMMARY EXECUTIONS

Effective prevention and investigation of extra-legal,
arbitrary and summary executions

The Economic and Social Council,*

Recalling that article 3 of the Universal Declaration of Human
Rights a/ [108] proclaims that everyone has the right to life, liberty and
security of person,

Bearing in mind that paragraph 1 of article 6 of the International
Covenant on Civil and Political Rights b/ [114] states that every human being
has an inherent right to life, that that right shall be protected by law and
that no one shall be arbitrarily deprived of his or her life,

Also bearing in mind the general comments of the Human Rights Committee
on the right to life as enunciated in article 6 of the International Covenant
on Civil and Political Rights,

Stressing that extra-legal, arbitrary and summary executions contravene
the human rights and fundamental freedoms proclaimed in the Universal
Declaration of Human Rights,

Mindful that the Seventh United Nations Congress on the Prevention of
Crime and the Treatment of Offenders, in resolution 11 on extra-legal,
arbitrary and summary executions, c/ [93] called upon all Governments to take
urgent and incisive action to investigate such acts, wherever they may occur,
to punish those found guilty and to take all other measures necessary to
prevent those practices,

Mindful also that the Economic and Social Council, in section VI of its
resolution 1986/10 of 21 May 1986, requested the Committee on Crime Prevention
and Control to consider at its tenth session the question of extra-legal,
arbitrary and summary executions with a view to elaborating principles on the
effective prevention and investigation of such practices,

Recalling that the General Assembly in its resolution 33/173 of
20 December 1978 expressed its deep concern at reports from various parts of
the world relating to enforced or involuntary disappearances and called upon
Governments, in the event of such reports, to take appropriate measures to
searching for such persons and to undertake speedy and impartial investigations,

Noting with appreciation the efforts of non-governmental organizations to
develop standards for investigations, d/ [115]

Note: References are numbered a/, b/ etc., with the original numbering
from the resolution given in square brackets immediately following the
footnote indicators.

*Resolution 1989/65 of 24 May 1989.

Emphasizing that the General Assembly in its resolution 42/141 of
7 December 1987 strongly condemned once again the large number of summary or
arbitrary executions, including extra-legal executions, that continued to take
place in various parts of the world,

Noting that in the same resolution the General Assembly recognized the
need for closer co-operation between the Centre for Human Rights, the Crime
Prevention and Criminal Justice Branch of the Centre for Social Development
and Humanitarian Affairs and the Committee on Crime Prevention and Control in
an effort to bring to an end summary or arbitrary executions,

Aware that effective prevention and investigation of extra-legal,
arbitrary and summary executions requires the provision of adequate financial
and technical resources,

1. Recommends that the Principles on the Effective Prevention and
Investigation of Extra-legal, Arbitrary and Summary Executions annexed to the
present resolution shall be taken into account and respected by Governments
within the framework of their national legislation and practices, and shall be
brought to the attention of law enforcement and criminal justice officials,
military personnel, lawyers, members of the executive and legislative bodies
of the Government and the public in general;

2. Requests the Committee on Crime Prevention and Control to keep the
above recommendations under constant review, including implementation of the
Principles, taking into account the various socio-economic, political and
cultural circumstances in which extra-legal, arbitrary and summary executions
occur;

3. Invites Member States that have not yet ratified or acceded to international instruments that prohibit extra-legal, arbitrary and summary executions, including the International Covenant on Civil and Political Rights, b/
[114] the Optional Protocol to the International Covenant on Civil and
Political Rights and the Convention against Torture and Other Cruel, Inhuman
or Degrading Treatment or Punishment, e/ [116] to become parties to these
instruments;

4. Requests the Secretary-General to include the Principles in the
United Nations publication entitled Human Rights: A Compilation of International Instruments;

5. Requests the United Nations regional and interregional institutes for
the prevention of crime and the treatment of offenders to give special attention in their research and training programmes to the Principles, and to the
International Covenant on Civil and Political Rights, b/ [114] the provisions
of the Convention against Torture and Other Cruel, Inhuman or Degrading
Treatment or Punishment, e/ [116] the Code of Conduct for Law Enforcement
Officials, f/ [104] the Declaration of Basic Principles of Justice for Victims
of Crime and Abuse of Power g/ [102] and other international instruments
relevant to the question of extra-legal, arbitrary and summary executions.

Annex to the Economic and Social Council resolution 1989/65

PRINCIPLES ON THE EFFECTIVE PREVENTION AND INVESTIGATION
OF EXTRA-LEGAL, ARBITRARY AND SUMMARY EXECUTIONS

Prevention

1. Governments shall prohibit by law all extra-legal, arbitrary and summary executions and shall ensure that any such executions are recognized as offences under their criminal laws, and are punishable by appropriate penalties which take into account the seriousness of such offences. Exceptional circumstances including a state of war or threat of war, internal political instability or any other public emergency may not be invoked as a justification of such executions. Such executions shall not be carried out under any circumstances including, but not limited to, situations of internal armed conflict, excessive or illegal use of force by a public official or other person acting in an official capacity or a person acting at the instigation, or with the consent or acquiescence of such person, and situations in which deaths occur in custody. This prohibition shall prevail over decrees issued by governmental authority.

2. In order to prevent extra-legal, arbitrary and summary executions, Governments shall ensure strict control, including a clear chain of command over all officials responsible for the apprehension, arrest, detention, custody and imprisonment as well as those officials authorized by law to use force and firearms.

3. Governments shall prohibit orders from superior officers or public author-ities authorizing or inciting other persons to carry out any such extra-legal, arbitrary or summary executions. All persons shall have the right and the duty to defy such orders. Training of law enforcement officials shall emphasize the above provisions.

4. Effective protection through judicial or other means shall be guaranteed to individuals and groups who are in danger of extra-legal, arbitrary or summary executions, including those who receive death threats.

5. No one shall be involuntarily returned or extradited to a country where there are substantial grounds for believing that he or she may become a victim of extra-legal, arbitrary or summary execution in that country.

6. Governments shall ensure that persons deprived of their liberty are held in officially recognized places of custody, and that accurate information on their custody and whereabouts, including transfers, is made promptly available to their relatives and lawyer or other persons of confidence.

7. Qualified inspectors, including medical personnel, or an equivalent independent authority, shall conduct inspections in places of custody on a regular basis, and be empowered to undertake unannounced inspections on their own initiative, with full guarantees of independence in the exercise of this function. The inspectors shall have unrestricted access to all persons in such places of custody, as well as to all their records.

8. Governments shall make every effort to prevent extra-legal, arbitrary and summary executions through measures such as diplomatic intercession, improved access of complainants to intergovernmental and judicial bodies, and public denunciation. Intergovernmental mechanisms shall be used to investigate reports of any such executions and to take effective action against such

practices. Governments, including those of countries where extra-legal, arbitrary and summary executions are reasonably suspected to occur, shall co-operate fully in international investigations on the subject.

Investigation

9.   There shall be a thorough, prompt and impartial investigation of all suspected cases of extra-legal, arbitrary and summary executions, including cases where complaints by relatives or other reliable reports suggest unnatural death in the above circumstances. Governments shall maintain investigative offices and procedures to undertake such inquiries. The purpose of the investigation shall be to determine the cause, manner and time of death, the person responsible, and any adequate autopsy, collection and analysis of all physical and documentary evidence, and statements from witnesses. The investigation shall distinguish between natural death, accidental death, suicide and homicide.

10.   The investigative authority shall have the power to obtain all the information necessary to the inquiry. Those persons conducting the investigation shall have at their disposal all the necessary budgetary and technical resources for effective investigation. They shall also have the authority to oblige officials allegedly involved in any such executions to appear and testify. The same shall apply to any witness. To this end, they shall be entitled to issue summons to witnesses, including the officials allegedly involved, and to demand the production of evidence.

11.   In cases in which the established investigative procedures are inadequate because of lack of expertise or impartiality, because of the importance of the matter or because of the apparent existence of a pattern of abuse, and in cases where there are complaints from the family of the victim about these inadequacies or other substantial reasons, Governments shall pursue investigations through an independent commission of inquiry or similar procedure. Members of such a commission shall be chosen for their recognized impartiality, competence and independence as individuals. In particular, they shall be independent of any institution, agency or person that may be the subject of the inquiry. The commission shall have the authority to obtain all information necessary to the inquiry and shall conduct the inquiry as provided for under these Principles.

12.   The body of the deceased person shall not be disposed of until an adequate autopsy is conducted by a physician, who shall, if possible, be an expert in forensic pathology. Those conducting the autopsy shall have the right of access to all investigative data, to the place where the body was discovered, and to the place where the death is thought to have occurred. If the body has been buried and it later appears that an investigation is required, the body shall be promptly and competently exhumed for an autopsy. If skeletal remains are discovered, they should be carefully exhumed and studied according to systematic anthropological techniques.

13.   The body of the deceased shall be available to those conducting the autopsy for a sufficient amount of time to enable a thorough investigation to be carried out. The autopsy shall, at a minimum, attempt to establish the identity of the deceased and the cause and manner of death. The time and place of death shall also be determined to the extent possible. Detailed colour photographs of the deceased shall be included in the autopsy report in order to document and support the findings of the investigation. The autopsy report must describe any and all injuries to the deceased including any evidence of torture.

14. In order to ensure objective results, those conducting the autopsy must be able to function impartially and independently of any potentially implicated persons or organizations or entities.

15. Complainants, witnesses, those conducting the investigation and their families shall be protected from violence, threats of violence or any other form of intimidation. Those potentially implicated in extra-legal, arbitrary or summary executions shall be removed from any position of control or power, whether direct or indirect, over complainants, witnesses and their families, as well as over those conducting investigations.

16. Families of the deceased and their legal representatives shall be informed of, and have access to, any hearing as well as to all information relevant to the investigation, and shall be entitled to present other evidence. The family of the deceased shall have the right to insist that a medical or other qualified representative be present at the autopsy. When the identity of a deceased person has been determined, a notification of death shall be posted, and the family or relatives of the deceased immediately informed. The body of the deceased shall be returned to them upon completion of the investigation.

17. A written report shall be made within a reasonable period of time on the methods and findings of such investigations. The report shall be made public immediately and shall include the scope of the inquiry, procedures and methods used to evaluate evidence as well as conclusions and recommendations based on findings of fact and on applicable law. The report shall also describe in detail specific events that were found to have occurred, and the evidence upon which such findings were based, and list the names of witnesses who testified, with the exception of those whose identities have been withheld for their own protection. The Government shall, within a reasonable period of time, either reply to the report of the investigation, or indicate the steps to be taken in response to it.

Legal proceedings

18. Governments shall ensure that persons identified by the investigation as having participated in extra-legal, arbitrary and summary executions in any territory under their jurisdiction are brought to justice. Governments shall either bring such persons to justice or co-operate to extradite any such persons to other countries wishing to exercise jurisdiction. This principle shall apply irrespective of who and where the perpetrators or the victims are, their nationalities or where the offence was committed.

19. Without prejudice to Principle 3 above, an order from a superior officer or a public authority may not be invoked as a justification for extra-legal, arbitrary or summary executions. Superiors, officers or other public officials may be held responsible for acts committed by officials under their hierarchical authority if they had a reasonable opportunity to prevent such acts. In no circumstances, including a state of war, siege or other public emergency, shall blanket immunity from prosecution be granted to any person allegedly involved in extra-legal, arbitrary or summary executions.

20. The families and dependents of victims of extra-legal, arbitrary and summary executions shall be entitled to fair and adequate compensation within a reasonable period of time.

Notes

a/ General Assembly resolution 217 A (III).

b/   See General Assembly resolution 2200 A (XXI), annex.

c/ See Seventh United Nations Congress on the Prevention of Crime and the Treatment of Offenders, Milan, 26 August-6 September 1985: report prepared by the Secretariat (United Nations publication, Sales No. E.86.IV.1), chap. I, sect. E.

d/ See E/AC.57/1988/NGO.4.

e/ General Assembly resolution 39/46, annex.

f/ General Assembly resolution 34/169, annex.

g/ General Assembly resolution 40/34, annex.

Annex II

POSTMORTEM DETECTION OF TORTURE

Torture technique	Physical findings
Beating	
1. General	Scars. Bruises. Lacerations. Multiple fractures at different stages of healing, especially in unusual locations, which have not been medically treated.
2. To the soles of the feet ("falanga", "falaka", "bastinado"), or fractures of the bones of the feet.	Haemorrhage in the soft tissues of the soles of the feet and ankles. Aseptic necrosis.
3. With the palms on both ears simultaneously ("el telefone").	Ruptured or scarred tympanic membranes. Injuries to external ear.
4. On the abdomen, while lying on a table with the upper half of the body unsupported ("operating table", "el quirofano").	Bruises on the abdomen. Back injuries. Ruptured abdominal viscera.
5. To the head.	Cerebral cortical atrophy. Scars. Skull fractures. Bruises. Haematomas.
Suspension	
6. By the wrists ("la bandera").	Bruises or scars about the wrists. Joint injuries.
7. By the arms or neck.	Bruises or scars at the site of binding. Prominent lividity in the lower extremities.
8. By the ankles ("murcielago").	Bruises or scars about the ankles. Joint injuries.
9. Head down, from a horizontal pole placed under the knees with the wrists bound to the ankles ("parrot's perch", "Jack", "pau de arara").	Bruises or scars on the anterior forearms and backs of the knees. Marks on the wrists and ankles.

Near suffocation

10. Forced immersion of head in water, often contaminated "wet submarine", "pileta", "Latina").

Faecal material or other debris in the mouth, pharynx, trachea, esophagus or lungs. Intrathoracic petechiae. Intra-thoracic petechiae.

11. Tying of a plastic bag over the head ("dry submarine").

Intro-thoracic petechiae.

Sexual abuse

12. Sexual abuse

Sexually transmitted diseases. Pregnancy. Injuries to breasts, external genitalia, vagina, anus or rectum.

Forced posture

13. Prolonged standing ("el planton").

Dependent edema. Petechiae in lower extremities.

14. Forced straddling of a bar ("saw horse", "el cabellete").

Perineal or scrotal haematomas.

Electric shock

15. Cattle prod ("la picana").

Burns: appearance depends on the age of the injury. Immediately: red spots, vesicles, and/or black exudate. Within a few weeks: circular, reddish, macular scars. At several months: small, white, reddish or brown spots resembling telangiectasias.

16. Wires connected to a source of electricity.

17. Heated metal skewer inserted into the anus ("black slave").

Peri-anal or rectal burns.

Miscellaneous

18. Dehydration

Vitreous humor electrolyte abnormalities.

Animal bites
(spiders, insects, rats, mice, dogs)

Bite marks.

Annex III

DRAWINGS OF PARTS OF HUMAN BODY FOR IDENTIFICATION OF TORTURE

MARK ALL EXISTING RESTORATIONS AND MISSING TEETH ON THIS CHART

Estimated   Age _____
Sex _____
Race _____

RIGHT | 1 2 3 4 5 6 7 8 9 10 11 12 13 1 15 16 | LEFT
32 31 30 29 28 27 26 25 24 23 22 21 20 19 18 17

Circle descriptive term

Prosthetic Appliances Present

Maxilla

Full Denture
Partial Denture
Fixed Bridge

Mandible

Full Denture
Partial Denture
Fixed Bridge

Describe completely all Prosthetic Appliances or Fixed Bridges _____

_____

_____

_____

_____

_____

Stains on teeth

Slight
Moderate
Severe

MARK ALL CARIES ON THIS CHART

Outline all caries and 'X' out all missing teeth

RIGHT | 1 2 3 4 5 6 7 8 9 10 11 12 13 14 15 16 | LEFT
32 31 30 29 28 27 26 25 24 23 22 21 20 19 18 17

Circle descriptive term

Relationship

Normal
Undershot
Overbite

Periodontal Condition

Excellent
Average
Poor

Calculus

Slight
Moderate
Severe

V. COMPARISON OF BODY WITH POSSIBLE DECEDENTS

NAMES OF DECEDENTS

TRAITS	BODY											
SEX												
AGE												
RACE												
STATURE												
WEIGHT												
CLOTHING												
JEWELLERY												
DOCUMENTS												
SCARS, TATTOOS												
OLD SURGERY												
ANOMALIES/DEFORM												
DENTITION												
FINGERPRINTS												
OTHER												
RULE OUT												
POSSIBLE BY EXCLUSION												
PROBABLE												
POSITIVE												

VI. NOTES

FULL BODY, FEMALE — LATERAL VIEW

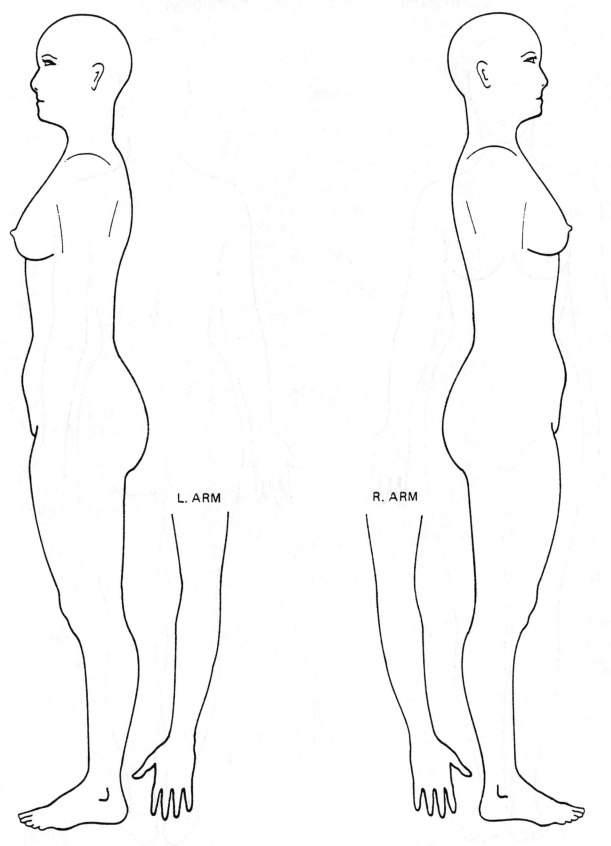

L. ARM

R. ARM

Name _____ Case No. _____

Date _____

FULL BODY, FEMALE – ANTERIOR AND POSTERIOR VIEWS

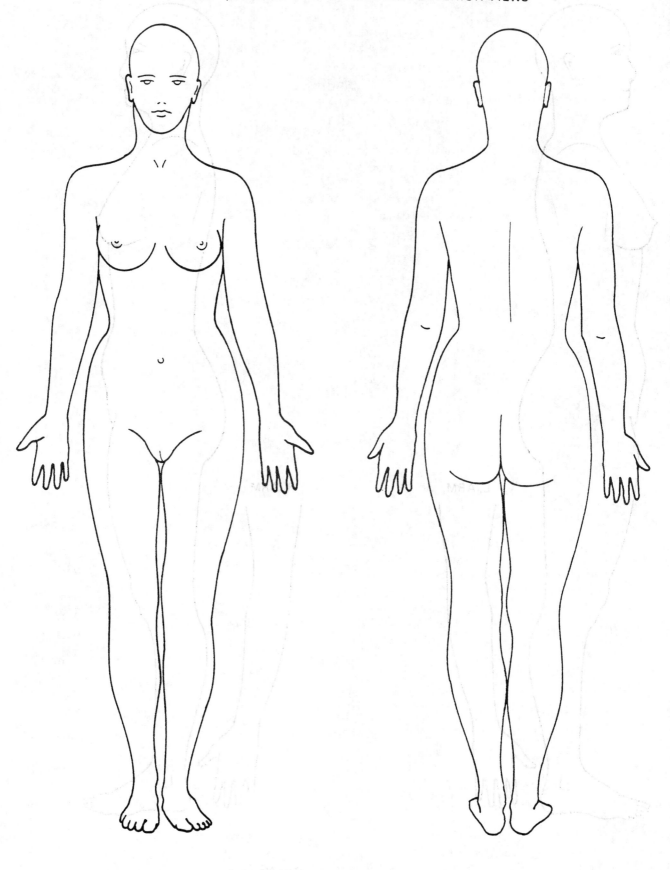

Name _____   Case No. _____

Date _____

THORACIC ABDOMINAL, FEMALE – ANTERIOR AND POSTERIOR VIEWS

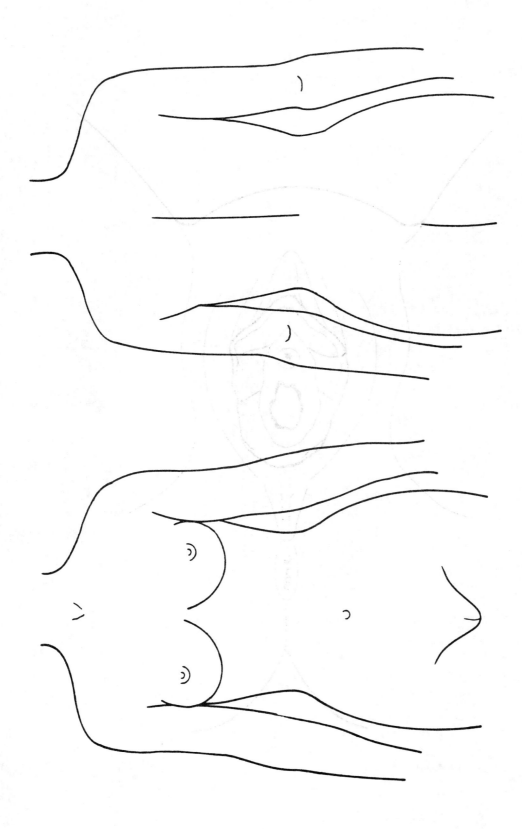

Name _____ Case No. _____

Date _____

PERINEUM – FEMALE

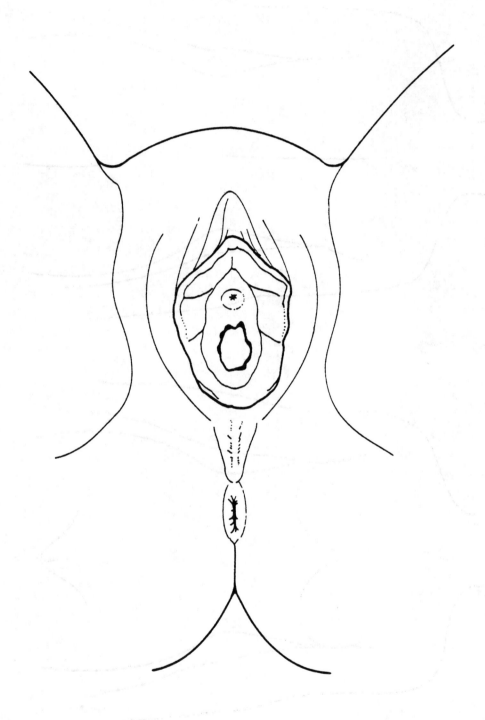

Name _____ Case No. _____

Date _____

FULL BODY, MALE – LATERAL VIEW

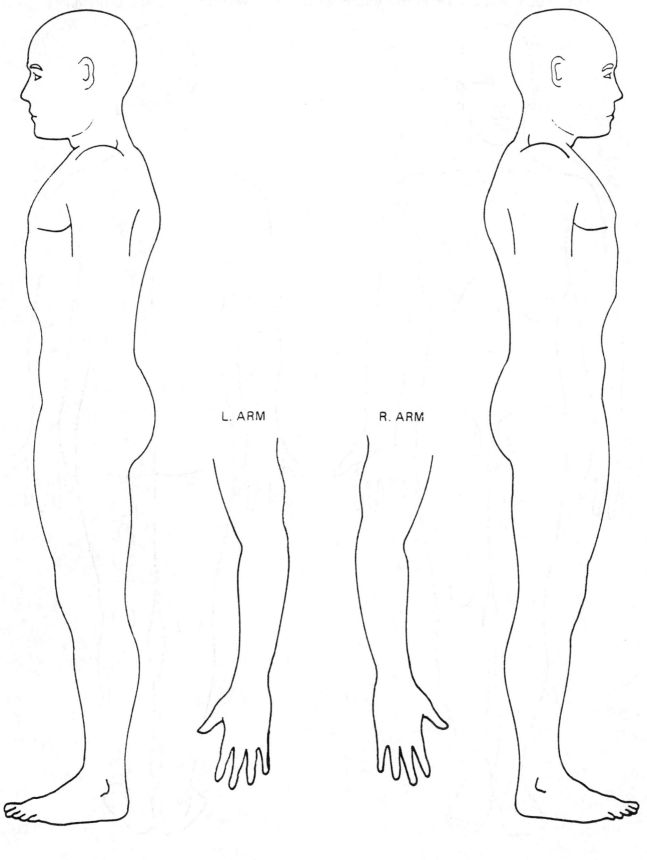

L. ARM   R. ARM

Name _____   Case No. _____

Date _____

FULL BODY, MALE – ANTERIOR AND POSTERIOR VIEWS (VENTRAL AND DORSAL)

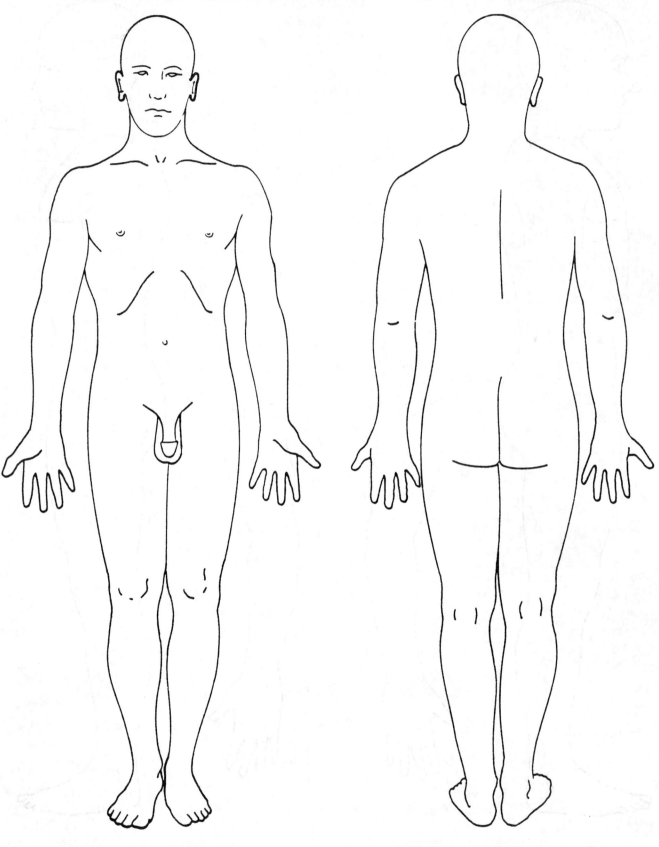

Name _____ Case No. _____

Date _____

THORACIC ABDOMINAL, MALE – ANTERIOR AND POSTERIOR VIEWS

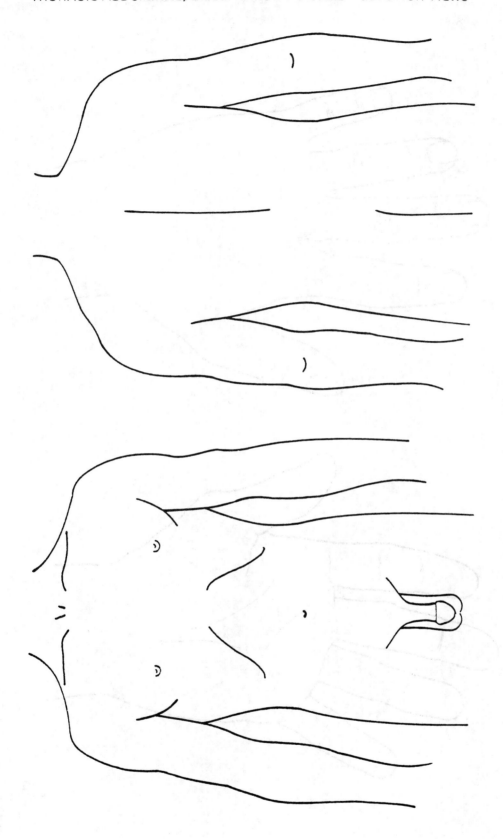

Name _____ Case No. _____

Date _____

RIGHT HAND – PALMAR AND DORSAL

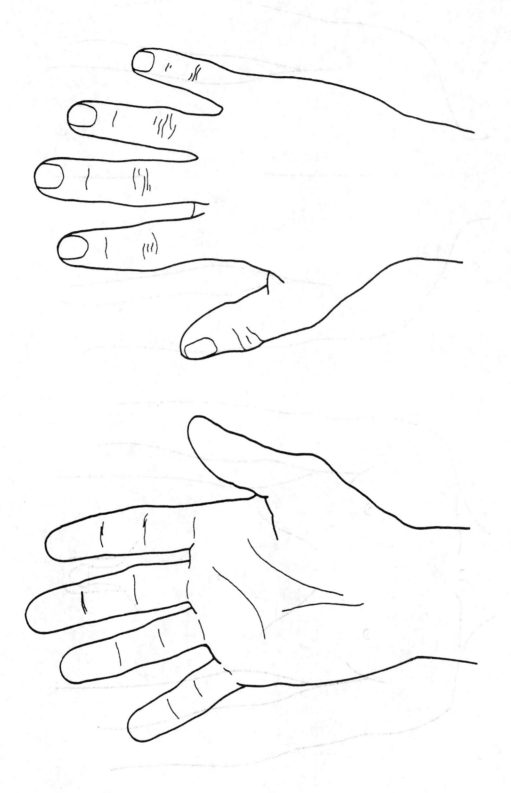

Name _____   Case No. _____

Date _____

LEFT HAND – PALMAR AND DORSAL

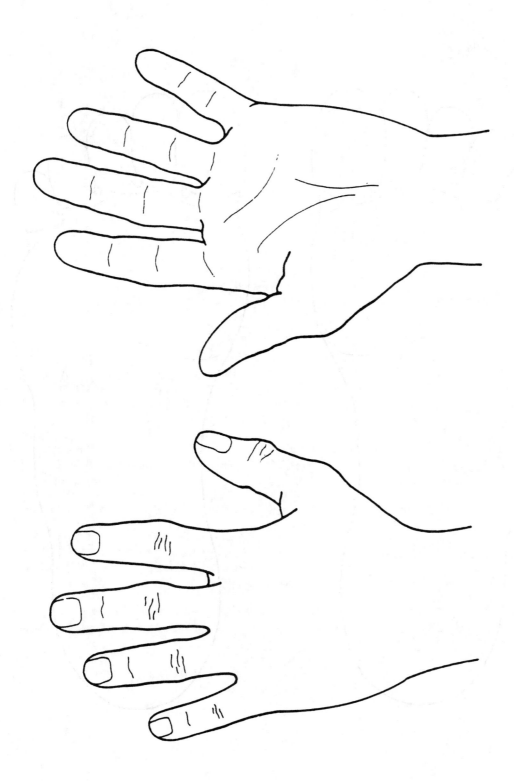

Name _____ Case No. _____

Date _____

FEET – LEFT AND RIGHT PLANTAR SURFACES

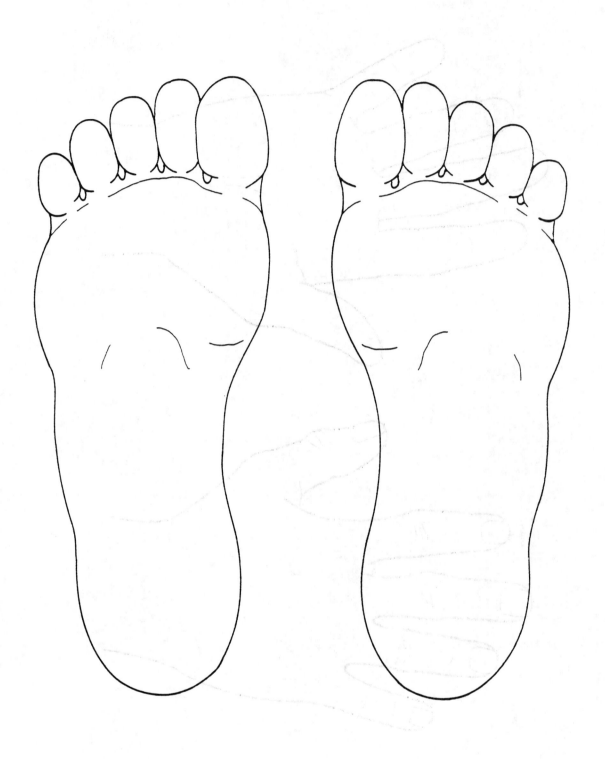

Name _____ Case No. _____

Date _____

INFANT – VENTRAL, DORSAL, AND LEFT AND RIGHT LATERAL VIEWS

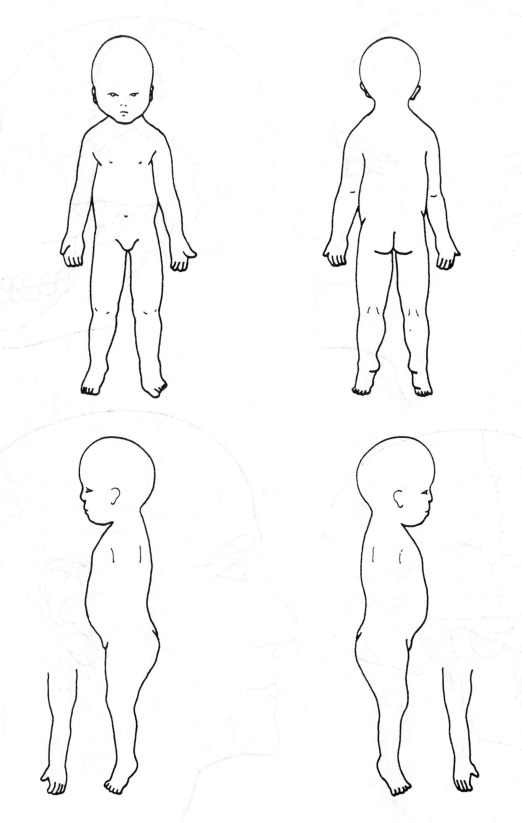

Name _____ Case No. _____

Date _____

HEAD – SURFACE AND SKELETAL ANATOMY, LATERAL VIEW

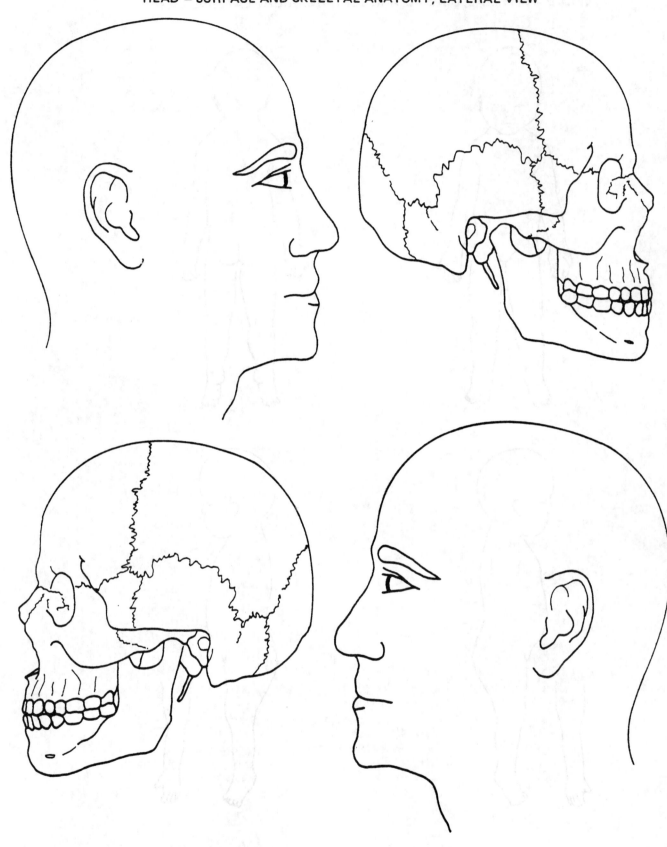

Name _____ Case No. _____

Date _____

SKELETON – ANTERIOR AND POSTERIOR VIEWS

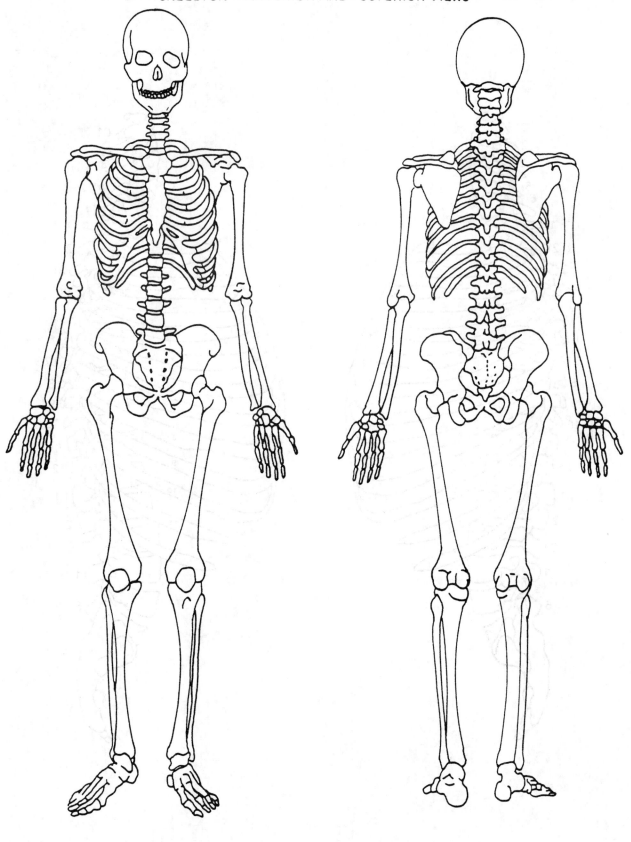

Name _____ Case No. _____

Date _____

VERTEBRAL COLUMN AND RIB CAGE – LEFT AND RIGHT LATERAL VIEWS

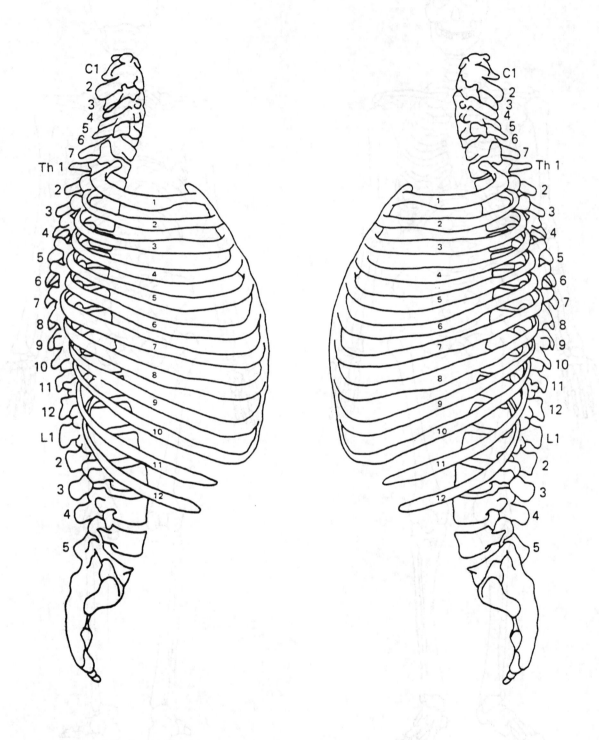

Name _____   Case No. _____

Date _____

HEAD — SURFACE AND SKELETAL ANATOMY, ANTERIOR AND POSTERIOR VIEWS

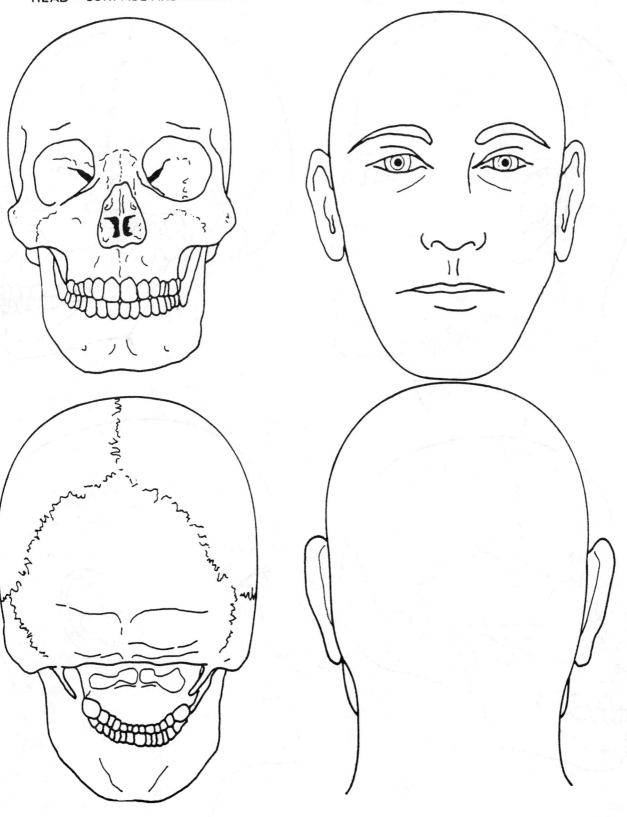

Name _____ Case No. _____

Date _____

HEAD – SURFACE AND SKELETAL ANATOMY, LATERAL VIEW

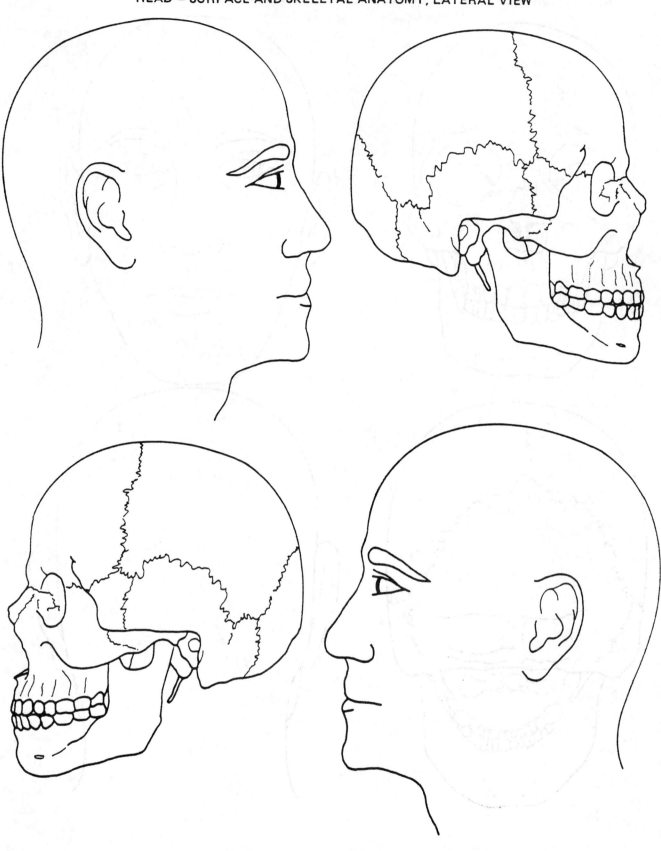

Name _____ Case No. _____

Date _____

HEAD – SURFACE AND SKELETAL ANATOMY, SUPERIOR VIEW – INFERIOR VIEW OF NECK

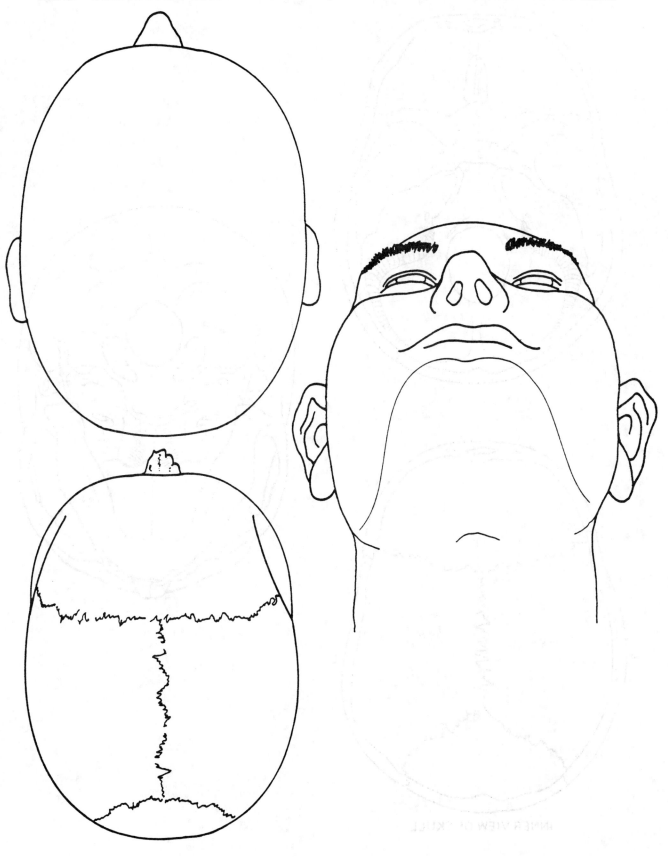

Name _____   Case No. _____

Date _____

SKULL – BASE, INFERIOR AND SUPERIOR VIEWS (PLUS CALVARIUM)

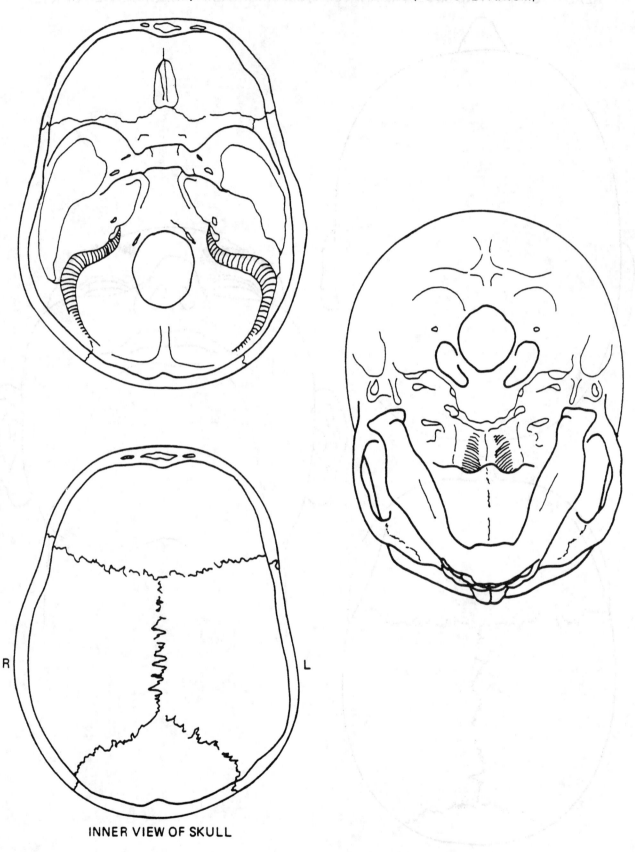

INNER VIEW OF SKULL

Name _____

Case No. _____

Date _____

BRAIN — SUPERIOR, INFERIOR, AND LATERAL VIEWS

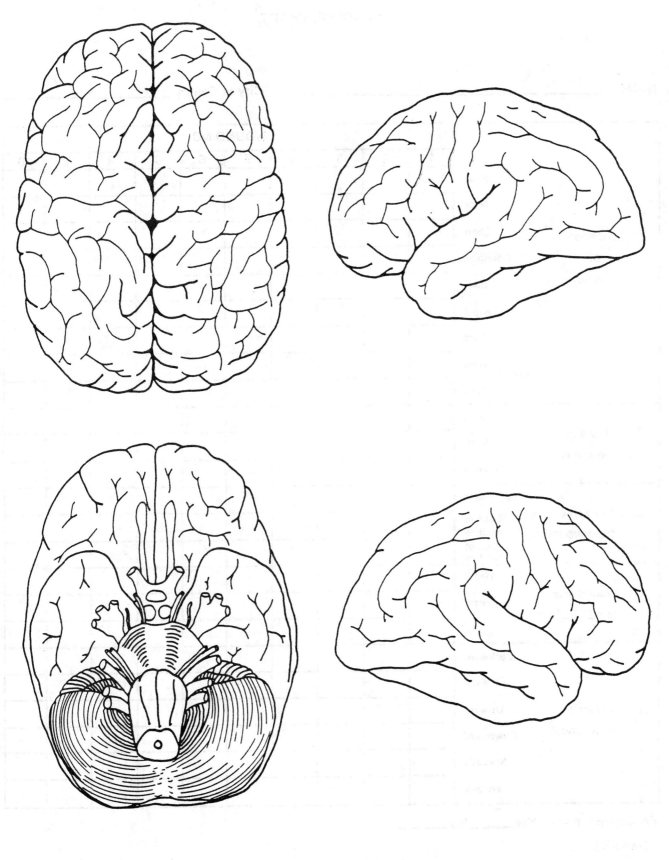

Name _____

Case No. _____

Date _____

STAB WOUND CHART

NAME _____ City or County _____

		1	2	3	4	5	6	7	8	9	10
						WOUND NO.					
1. Location of wound:	Head										
	Neck										
	Chest										
	Abdomen										
	Back										
	Arm < Right										
	Left										
	Leg < Right										
	Left										
2. The skin wound is:	Horiz.										
	Vert.										
	Oblique										
3. Centimetres from wound to:	Top of head										
	Right of midline										
	Left of midline										
4. Wound size in millimetres	Width										
	Length										
	Diam.										
5. Direction of wound:	Backward										
	Forward										
	Upward										
	Downward										
	Medially										
	Laterally										

Photographs made: Yes_____ No _____

REMARKS:

Examined by: _____ Date: _____

FIREARM WOUND CHART

NAME _____ CASE NO. _____

		1		2		3		4		5		6	
		Ent.	Ex.	Ent.	Ex.	Ent.	Ex.	Ent.	Ex.	Ent.	Ex.	Ent.	Ex.
1. Location of wound:	Head												
	Neck												
	Chest												
	Abdomen												
	Back												
Arm <	Right												
	Left												
Leg <	Right												
	Left												
2. Size of wound: (Centimetres)	Diam.												
	Width												
	Length												
3. Centimetres from wound to:	Top of head												
	Right of midline												
	Left of midline												
4. Firearm Residue:	On skin												
	Clothing												
	Absent												
5. Direction of missile through body:	Backward												
	Forward												
	Downward												
	Upward												
	To right												
	To left												
6. Missile Recovered:	Probable Calibre												
	Shotgun												

Photographs: _____   X-rays: _____

REMARKS:

Examiner: _____ Date: _____